From Passion to Execution:

How to Start and Grow an Effective Nonprofit Organization

Lyn Scott

Course Technology PTR

A part of Cengage Learning

COURSE TECHNOLOGY
CENGAGE Learning·

Australia • Brazil • Japan • Korea • Mexico • Singapore • Spain • United Kingdom • United States

COURSE TECHNOLOGY
CENGAGE Learning·

From Passion to Execution: How to Start and Grow an Effective Nonprofit Organization
Lyn Scott

Publisher and General Manager, Course Technology PTR:
Stacy L. Hiquet

Associate Director of Marketing:
Sarah Panella

Manager of Editorial Services:
Heather Talbot

Senior Marketing Manager:
Mark Hughes

Senior Acquisitions Editor:
Mitzi Koontz

Project Editor:
Jenny Davidson

Copy Editor:
Sara Gullion

Interior Layout:
Jill Flores

Cover Designer:
Luke Fletcher

Indexer:
Sharon Shock

Proofreader:
Mike Beady

For product information and technology assistance, contact us at
Cengage Learning Customer & Sales Support, 1-800-354-9706
For permission to use material from this text or product,
submit all requests online at **cengage.com/permissions**
Further permissions questions can be emailed to
permissionrequest@cengage.com

NOTE TO THE READER
The reader is notified that this text is best viewed as a general educational tool. Disparity between jurisdictions and ongoing changes in technology and laws, codes, and regulations will require the reader to have current knowledge of local laws and practices. Qualified professional advice should be sought when necessary.

All trademarks are the property of their respective owners.

All images © Cengage Learning unless otherwise noted.

Library of Congress Control Number: 2012930795

ISBN-13: 978-1-4354-6012-6

ISBN-10: 1-4354-6012-X

Course Technology, a part of Cengage Learning
20 Channel Center Street
Boston, MA 02210
USA

Cengage Learning is a leading provider of customized learning solutions with office locations around the globe, including Singapore, the United Kingdom, Australia, Mexico, Brazil, and Japan. Locate your local office at: **international.cengage.com/region**

Cengage Learning products are represented in Canada by Nelson Education, Ltd. For your lifelong learning solutions, visit **courseptr.com** Visit our corporate Web site at **cengage.com**

Printed by RR Donnelley. Crawfordsville, IN. 1st Ptg. 03/2012
Printed in the United States of America
1 2 3 4 5 6 7 14 13 12

To Ashley

*In a perfect world, it would be all about
rainbows and ponies.*

Acknowledgments

Special thanks to my family and friends and the team from Course PTR.

About the Author

Lyn Scott currently serves as Vice President/CFO of Tarrant County Samaritan Housing, Inc. The social service organization provides supportive services and housing for its clients. Additionally, Ms. Scott served as Chief Operating Officer of a nationally chartered history museum and educational institution. With a career focus in business operations, her extensive professional experience encompasses banking, defense/manufacturing, and nonprofit organizations.

Scott's affiliations and honors include: member of the Smithsonian Institution Affiliations Advisory Council; 2010 Power Pipeline Committee of the Board; member of the American Association of University Women, Tarrant County; Member of Executive Women International, Dallas; member of the Certified Fraud Examiners; TWU Phi Kappa Phi; Leadership Texas, Class of '09; Scholar in Residence for Durham Museum; and, recently featured in Cadillac's Spirit of Texas.

Scott is a graduate of Texas Wesleyan University, and recently received her MBA from Texas Woman's University. Driven by a passion for volunteerism and community activism, Lyn has held volunteer positions at several local charities. Lyn resides in Arlington, Texas, with her husband, Jeff, and 18-year-old daughter, Ashley.

Contributors

F ran Lobpries, CFRE
Certified Fund Raising Executive

Fran Lobpries has over twenty years of fund development experience with special emphasis in Strategic Integrated Development Planning and Implementation. Having raised millions of dollars annually through annual fund, major gift, and capital campaigns, Lobpries finds her communication skills to be key to her success. From grants, letters, videos, and newsletters, telling your story in ways that are meaningful to your audiences are among her artful trademarks.

Lobpries provides a range of development consulting, facilitating, and training services including: strategic planning, development, best-practices audit report, development program annual plan, stewardship plan, communications plan, major gifts program in conjunction with Raiser's Edge Moves Management, volunteer program plan, and planned giving campaign plan.

Having served as development director and executive director for a number of organizations including Archer Area Fund of Communities Foundation of Texas, The Women's Museum, and Presbyterian Communities and Services Foundation, Lobpries understands the demands and aspirations of the development shop. As a consultant, she is able to bring an outsider's perspective and a "tool-kit" of new ideas into focus for daily application in your reality.

As a member of the Association of Fundraising Professionals, Lobpries has led the CFRE Review Course for the Dallas Chapter for the past eight years. The CFRE designation is awarded by the National Organization for Competency Assurance to those who have passed an extensive test and other assurances equivalent to the CPA for accountants. Receiving her credential in 2002, Lobpries was selected to participate in the International CFRE Leadership program in Toronto, Canada. Lobpries also supports her professional organization as a committee member of the National Philanthropy Day awards luncheon for the past eight years. Most recently, Lobpries served on a sub-committee for the selection of AFP International's Philanthropist of the Year award.

A graduate of Leadership Texas and Leadership America, Lobpries most enjoys cultivating new generations of leaders, particularly within the non profit community.

Lobpries resides in Dallas, Texas, with her husband, Mike. She is the mother of three and the "Nana- Franna" to seven wonderful grandchildren. She may be reached at lobpries1@sbcglobal.net.

 **Denita Powell Malvern** is a nonprofit professional with over fourteen years of museum and education experience. Her professional career includes serving as the Education Programs Manager at The Women's Museum: An Institute for the Future, Assistant Director of the College of Adult Learning for Cincinnati Christian University, Audience Research and Public Programs Manager for The National Underground Railroad Freedom Center, and Cincinnati Public Schools. Denita obtained her Bachelor of Arts in History from Wittenberg University and her M.Ed. in Education Administration from Xavier University.

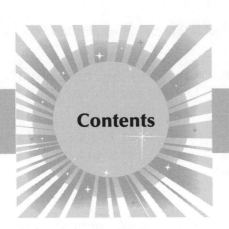

Contents

Introduction

According to the most recent statistics listed on the National Center for Charitable Statistics website, at the end of 2010 there were 1,617,301 charitable organizations registered with the Internal Revenue Service. Working together to improve our communities has long been part of the fabric of America. U.S. citizens' individual giving is consistently a higher percentage of GDP than most any other country.

As our global economy suffers from the after effects of a lingering recession and several large-scale natural disasters, our government agencies' budgets and services are stretched far beyond their limits. Many of us have personal safety nets to ensure our basic needs are met, yet we still have members of our communities who fall through the "cracks" in our services.

Together, I believe we can solve the most critical issues facing humankind. The emphasis must be on guaranteeing our brothers and sisters have the basic human right to thrive. It is my hope that this practical guide will provide you with the roadmap to open the doors to your new nonprofit, serving the greater good of our communities. I wish you every success with your new organization and I am personally grateful that you have chosen to actively participate in making the world a better place!

Part 1

Catch the Vision

Chapter 1

Passion, Possibilities, and Purpose: Gifts of Nonprofit Organizations

---

"Never doubt that a small group of committed citizens can change the world. Indeed, it is the only thing that ever has."

~Margaret Mead, Anthropologist

So you want to make a positive impact in the world? As Margaret Mead said, it has always been a band of individuals that improve the quality of life in our communities, even the world-at-large. The birth of an organization is typically the result of the entrepreneur's passion. In the case of nonprofit organizations, some unfortunately are a consequence of a tragic circumstance or event, for example, Mothers Against Drunk Driving or Susan G. Komen for the Cure. It is my desire that this book will provide readers with an overview and examples of how passion and drive can become a possibility with a purpose. You, too, have what it takes to be a social entrepreneur.

This book will highlight several grassroots, start-up charitable organizations to give you varying perspectives of the process. You will learn about these amazing nonprofits, their missions, and the challenges they have overcome since incorporating.

Not every organization or business purpose qualifies as a charitable cause. At this point, you should be asking, what qualifies as a nonprofit organization? Most important is the Internal Revenue Service's official description, which in part states that an exempt organization is organized and operated exclusively for exempt purposes set forth in section code 501(c)(3), and none of the organization's earnings may inure any private shareholder or individual. Additionally, the organization's primary purpose cannot be an attempt to change legislation (established primarily for lobbying). Exempt purposes, according to the IRS, include charitable, religious, educational, scientific, literary, public safety testing, fostering national or international amateur sports competition, and preventing cruelty to children or animals. The IRS further defines charity as relief of the poor, the distressed, or the underprivileged; advancement of religion; advancement of education or science; erecting or maintaining public buildings, monuments, or works; lessening the burdens of government; lessening neighborhood tensions; eliminating prejudice and discrimination; defending human and civil rights secured by law; and combating community deterioration and juvenile delinquency (Exemption Requirements—Section 501(c)(3) Organizations).

The IRS tax-exempt code is organized by the qualifying organization's business purpose. The table on the next page provides an overview of the different types of exempt organizations.

The most important advantage of 501(c)(3) status is the ability to receive tax-deductible donations. Other advantages include tax exemptions, the ability to qualify for grants, and lower cost postage rates and filing fees. In addition, many service industries offer discounted rates for nonprofit organizations. These services often include banking fees, accounting services, and advertising rates.

Likewise, there are also disadvantages to structuring your new organization as a nonprofit. One important disadvantage is the loss of autonomous control. A nonprofit organization belongs to the public-at-large, so the operations and services must meet the public's expectations. Which leads us to yet another disadvantage—nonprofit organizations' financial records are required to be open to public inspection; this transparency allows for a great deal of scrutiny. The salaries of many large, national nonprofit organizations' executives have come under the microscope over the past few years. With the news of so many unscrupulous executives of both for-profit and nonprofit corporations, the public is a bit sensitive to the excesses in executive compensation packages. Other disadvantages to consider are the limited purposes outlined earlier and the expense limitation on lobbying activities intended to influence legislation.

Types of Exempt Organizations

IRS Tax Exempt Code Section	Purpose
501(c)(3)	Organized for charitable purposes as defined by the IRS
501(c)(4)	Civic leagues; Local employee associations; Social welfare organizations
501(c)(5)	Labor, agricultural, or horticultural organizations
501(c)(6)	Business leagues; Chambers of commerce
501(c)(7)	Recreational clubs; Social clubs
501(c)(9)	Voluntary employees' beneficiary associations
501(c)(10)	Domestic fraternal societies, orders, and lodges
501(c)(12)	Benevolent life insurance companies
501(c)(13)	Cemeteries, crematoria, etc.
501(c)(15)	Mutual insurance companies or associations (other than life or marine)
501(c)(17)	Employee associations; Trusts providing for the payment of supplemental unemployment benefits
501(c)(19)	Veterans organizations

Many nonprofits were started by accidental advocates. As a result of tragedy or perhaps circumstances beyond their control, people who are facing life-changing situations often realize that they are functioning in a black hole where there are no services designed to help in their particular situation. Passionate, purposeful people have the energy, boundless determination, and desire to change the world. As Margaret Mead's quote so eloquently states, small groups of citizens are what bring about positive change in our communities, both large and small.

Ten years ago, my husband's employment contract was unexpectedly terminated and we were emotionally and financially devastated. His job had provided our primary income and we had dipped into our savings for various wants and needs, so our cushion was virtually non-existent. After a few days of deep contemplation, an unconventional thought occurred to us—why not start a nonprofit to better serve our community? Of course, we continually questioned our decision. Could we? Should we? After six months of research, paperwork in duplicate and triplicate, and many a late night discussion, a new nonprofit was born. I assure you, if we can accomplish this lofty feat, so can you!

I must provide full disclosure. My husband and I had both worked for nonprofits, so we had a basic knowledge of the structure and operations of a charitable organization. Since our family's budget was suddenly dependent solely on my part-time income, we were not in any financial position to hire an attorney to complete the paperwork, so we called upon our friends (they accepted belly laughs and dinners for payment!) and our local library's resources to provide us with guidance and ultimately, the roadmap to fulfill our mission. It is my hope that this book will provide a basic guide and impetus for you to fulfill your goal of starting a nonprofit.

As our nation struggles through another extended economic recession, many of us are in desperate need of purposeful employment and realize that our government institutions are no longer equipped to adequately provide the much-needed services our communities require. I do not want to delude you; this process will be tedious, but certainly well worth your effort.

For some of us, there comes a time when we realize that our professional careers are not in line with our personal passions, our jobs are not making the world a better place to live, or just the fact that our talents are not being fully utilized. Do you believe that you have the power to make the world a better place? Sitting in traffic on a congested highway, have you thought of an unmet social need and an appropriate solution? Then it is time to harness your passion and have the faith to follow the process to execution—you can start your own nonprofit.

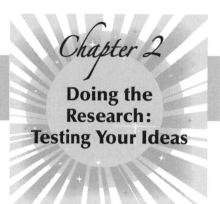

Chapter 2

Doing the Research: Testing Your Ideas

"Take the first step in faith. You don't have to see the whole staircase, just take the first step."

~Martin Luther King, Jr., Civil Rights Leader

Pat yourself on the back! You've taken the first step by deciding that you have what it takes to make the world a better place. Your passion is the key ingredient—the actual dynamite to ignite a social revolution. You needn't have all of the answers, but it is time to start using your business and marketing savvy in the second step.

As a social entrepreneur, you can envision the benefits that a thorough situation analysis will provide at this point. This is the stage in which you attempt to organize your ideas and really narrow down your business objectives. When reviewing the environment for your proposed nonprofit, you will want to analyze the external and the internal, as well as the customer (stakeholders) environment. This is similar to the basis for a business plan in for-profit companies.

Let's discuss the customer or stakeholder environment first of all. During this process you will explore if others need or will be interested in the services your organization will offer. Will your nonprofit serve a big portion of the population or just a targeted segment? How and where will the beneficiaries of your services receive them? Why do the recipients need/want the services and why may they choose to decline the services? You must ensure that your organization's proposed services will be in high demand and funders will want to support your mission.

After conducting the customer analysis, the situation analysis of the external environment will determine the "uniqueness" of your nonprofit. It is important to find out if there are any other organizations that are currently providing the services that you imagine your nonprofit organization will offer your community. Of course, this certainly would not prohibit you from opening your organization, but you will need to be prepared to compete for community support and funding. Other factors to explore would be the political trends; is there pending or proposed legislation that would apply to your planned organization? You would also want to do extensive research on the regulatory requirements for the type of organization and services that you plan to offer.

The last part of the situation analysis is a critical review of the internal environment. You should now have a better idea of your objectives and be able to answer the question of what problem or need your organization is solving. And finally, how will you raise the funds necessary to fulfill your mission? Will the organization be of interest to individual, foundation, corporate, and government funders? Just because the mission speaks to your heart, you must ensure that it speaks to the checkbooks of donors. Many important organizations never make it past the "idea" phase simply because a solid fundraising plan was not established early on in the life cycle of the nonprofit.

Your friends and family will give you valuable feedback regarding your organizational business plan. This initial test phase will give you honest information and will help refine your business plan and mission. Our friends and family were appropriately concerned about our unconventional plan in the beginning. They peppered us with questions of how we would be able to finance a start-up organization and provide a steady income for our family; were we qualified to file all of the required legal documents; is there a community need for the services we planned to provide?

All of these questions are valid and likely the same questions potential funders and donors would also have. This process gives you the opportunity to devise detailed and professional answers to the questions. Many entrepreneurs commit too little time conducting the situational analysis. This process requires putting your ideas in front of groups of people, asking for their feedback. The most difficult part may be listening to their criticisms of your passion. I assure you that developing a thick skin will be a big benefit to you as a nonprofit executive and your business plan will be airtight if you spend a sufficient amount of time conducting the analysis and allowing your idea to take on a concrete form. This process will give you a strategic advantage in developing a clear roadmap for collecting the most essential ingredients to start your organization.

I would like to introduce you to our first case study, Joy's House. The founder is Tina McIntosh and she is a wonderful example of commitment and determination. When she launched Joy's House, she cleaned houses to supplement her family's income since the initial budget did not allow for her salary. I am so impressed by her willingness to do whatever was required to make the organization a success and fulfill the needs of her community.

Case Study

Name of nonprofit organization: Joy's House

Address: 2028 E. Broad Ripple Avenue, Indianapolis, IN 46220

Phone: (317) 254-0828

Website: www.joyshouse.org

Date of incorporation: May 1999

Founder(s): Tina McIntosh, President & CEO

Inspiration: Tina's inspiration began when she volunteered at an adult day facility while in college in Muncie, Indiana. One woman, in particular, made a lasting impression on Tina. A few years later, Tina suffered several personal tragedies and feels that during this period God guided her and gave clarity to her purpose.

Background/community need: Tina's background and education have been beneficial since the organization's beginning. She visited other adult day service homes in her community, which strengthened her commitment to open a standalone, home life environment, not-for-profit organization.

Tina also tapped into her local community and was able to use another small business's needs assessment and demographic study to help shape her business plan. Her research confirmed that her community has a huge need for adult day services and expects the need to continue to grow as our population ages.

A catalyst for Tina is that she has been lucky to have always had older people in her life. She believes in following one's dreams and continually striving to make a difference in the lives of others.

Organization's mission: "Joy's House is committed to supporting families by providing exceptional adult day services. We assist our Guests by sharing an embracing, safe, and accepting environment while providing caregivers peace of mind, education, and ongoing understanding and encouragement."

Organization's vision: Joy's House strives to be the industry model for adult day services and to ensure that the Indianapolis community is aware of adult day services as a health care option.

Were the required filings completed internally or by an external expert? Tina was blessed to have an attorney join the initial group that had a hand in opening Joy's House. The attorney prepared all of the required documents pro bono and agreed to serve as the organization's first board chair.

Organizational challenges/solutions: Tina's challenge is two-fold—growth and time. As the organization served more Guests, more employees were needed to help meet the goals. Tina's passion is to care for people, not necessarily manage them. Like many others, Tina takes the responsibility of caring for her employees' stability very seriously. One lesson that she has learned is that she can't be everything to everyone at every moment.

Organizational successes: Some of the accomplishments that Tina is most proud of include the annual Gala, which attracted more than 350 supporters in 2011. As she stood in the middle of the room, Tina was amazed at the number of people that have chosen to be a part of Joy's House and who have been positively impacted by being involved.

Another accomplishment is that thousands of Guests, caregivers, volunteers, doctors, and families have been positively influenced by the impact of Joy's House.

Tina believes that when she recounts the highlights of her life, Joy's House will land toward the top of the list, along with her family and dear friends.

Furthermore, she feels blessed to be the seed of the organization that changes the lives of everyone that comes through the door of Joy's House.

Advice to others: Tina offers the following advice to others considering following their passion:

Nonprofit organizations require business savvy, just like for-profit businesses. If you do not have a business background, consider finding a volunteer that can supplement your skills to aid in the necessary planning, strategy, etc.

Make a conscious effort to stay true to your organization's mission. Tina and her staff meet at least annually to "cut out the fluff." When looking for creative ways to secure funding, many nonprofit organizations make the mistake of continually creating new programs that could potentially stray from the original mission. It is important to review your organization's mission and vision on a regular and ongoing basis to ensure that the services provided have a direct correlation to the mission.

Empowering employees is her second piece of advice. A strong leader needs to evaluate her team members' strengths, as well as the employees' career goals. The organization will also benefit from an employee's engagement and performance at or beyond their full potential. Likewise, there will be times when employees or volunteers will no longer be a good fit for either their position or the organization and it is okay, even encouraged, to support them as they find another opportunity outside of the organization.

And her last nugget of advice is to be honest with funders about a program's success. If the program did not meet the needs of her clients, Tina and her team feel it best to be honest with the funder so that the funder knows how to best support their organization, but also what may or may not work for other organizations in the future. Funders want to know that they are helping organizations to find their best through trials and errors. They need honesty to do this effectively. After all, Tina's philosophy is that funders are investors and the best practice is to always be forthcoming with information.

Chapter 3

Key Ingredients for Starting a Nonprofit Organization

"Some people give time, some money, some their skills and connections, some literally give their life's blood. But everyone has something to give."

~Barbara Bush, former First Lady

The key ingredients for starting a nonprofit organization are numerous and perhaps a bit hard to wrap your arms around. I have compiled the following checklist to help clarify the next steps in our process. This guide, combined with the Internet and its expansive resources, will be of great benefit to you at this point. Not only will you find helpful information from local, state, and federal government agencies' websites, you can also speed up your timetable immensely.

The following chapters and the sample forms in the last section of the book will give you detailed contact information for each state. Here is a general overview of the important personal skills and elements we have previously discussed and where we will go from here:

* Have passion.
* Use your marketing skills to develop a valid business plan along with a mission and solid service plan.
* Populate a productive and dedicated volunteer board of directors.
* Create a viable and sustainable funding plan.

* Raise available seed funding (most likely your personal resources).
* Choose your organization's name.
* Search federal trademarks at: http://www.uspto.gov/trademarks/index.jsp.
* Search available website addresses at: http://www.whois.com/.
* Use your Secretary of State's business search resource. (Each state's SOS contact information is found in the appendix.)
* Apply for incorporation as a nonprofit in your state (and any other state that your corporation will have operations). Contact information and current fee schedules at the time of publication are provided in the appendix.
* Apply for a Taxpayer Identification Number/Employer Identification Number (even if you do not plan to have employees yet).

  > You may request an EIN by:
  >
  > calling 1-800-829-4933,
  >
  > downloading the application form from http://www.irs.gov/pub/irs-pdf/fss4.pdf,
  >
  > or using the copy provided in the appendix.

* Apply for exempt status from the Internal Revenue Service, using the following information and forms:

  * Publication 557: Tax Exempt Status for your Organization
    http://www.irs.gov/pub/irs-pdf/p557.pdf
  * Publication 4220: Applying for 501(c)(3) Status
    http://www.irs.gov/pub/irs-pdf/p4220.pdf

* Develop Articles of Incorporation. (Sample provided in Chapter 9.)
* Create bylaws for your organization. (Sample provided in Chapter 6.)
* Hire dedicated and knowledgeable staff, volunteers, and board members. To fulfill your mission, you will need as many advocates and supporters that you can recruit and manage.

Hopefully, this list will help to clarify our next steps in the process. Although possible, it will be difficult for you to take on this major project alone. At this stage, you should begin to petition your colleagues, friends, and associates to join your organization during this crucial start-up phase. Chapter 5 provides an in-depth discussion of the elements in building a strong foundation for your organization and the importance of constructing a productive volunteer board as the first pillar.

At this point, I would like to introduce you to another case study of a recently organized nonprofit, NICU Helping Hands. This organization was started by a local foundation to serve the needs of families with premature babies. As you read the case study, you will see that Lisa Grubbs, president of the nonprofit, faces some of the same challenges as many other new corporations. The organization's numerous successes are a result of the devotion Lisa and her team has in fulfilling the mission of helping families affected by premature birth.

Case Study

Name of nonprofit organization: NICU Helping Hands Foundation

Address: 301 Commerce Street, Suite 3200, Fort Worth, Texas 76102

Website: www.nicuhelpinghands.org

Date of incorporation: October 2010

Founder(s): Once Upon a Time, a local area Foundation that supports educational and health-related initiatives, founded NICU Helping Hands to create a Fort Worth–based organization whose primary focus is to help premature babies. While there are other organizations that appear to do similar things, none of them are based locally with a commitment to take all dollars raised and put them back into our community, helping our babies.

Inspiration: Lisa Grubbs is President of the foundation, and she has spent many years seeing families experience the birth of a premature baby. Her husband is a neonatologist and it became apparent to Lisa that families in the NICU desperately need support services and educational opportunities when faced with the premature birth of a baby. About four and a half years ago, Lisa's dear friend had premature twins and it was a life-changing experience for the family, as well as their close friends. Lisa says that watching this family's experience up close motivated her to personally become involved in making a difference for families dealing with this medical crisis. She is inspired daily to continue serving in this area as Lisa watches her friend's beautiful little girls grow and deal with the long-term issues they have related to their premature births.

Background/community need: In 2006, 12% of all live births in the United States were pre-term (before 37 weeks gestation). For that year, the pre-term rate in Texas was 13.7%. In the Dallas–Fort Worth metropolitan area, Tarrant County saw a 2% overall increase between 2007 and 2008, although the overall volume of all Neonatal Intensive Care Units was declining. The primary county served by NICU Helping Hands has the highest rate of prematurity in the state of Texas and affected families need a local organization that will meet their needs both educationally and emotionally.

Organization's mission: NICU Helping Hands is an organization that develops hospital- and community-based projects that provide education and support to families of premature infants. Our mission is to provide comprehensive support programs and resources to parents of premature infants in our community, not only during their stay in the neonatal intensive care unit of a local hospital, but during and after their transition home.

Organization's vision: When a family in Tarrant County and the surrounding areas has a baby prematurely we want their family, friends, and co-workers to immediately think of NICU Helping Hands as the organization to contact to receive support and education from in their community.

Were the required filings completed internally or by an external expert? The required filings were completed and filed by internal members of the organization.

Organizational challenges/solutions: Like many start-up organizations, Lisa finds that it is a challenge to run an organization with little to no staff. They are working strategically to secure funding to increase their staff and also to expand their programs. NICU Helping Hands has been able to secure funding to start an in-hospital program (Project NICU) immediately, but they are continuing to raise funds that will allow the organization to grow into other areas in the community. It is also a challenge to get visibility and name recognition in the community when operating without a marketing staff. Lisa and her team are in the process of applying for grants, planning fundraisers for 2012, and networking through a variety of sources in the community that are interested in helping the organization grow.

Organizational successes: In a little over a year, NICU Helping Hands has successfully launched an in-hospital program (Project NICU) at Baylor All Saints in Fort Worth. The organization now has a full-time program facilitator available to serve families 40 hours a week in the Baylor All Saints NICU. NICU Helping Hands offers parent support and education, sibling support, memory archiving, ante-partum support, transportation support, bereavement support, and from hospital to home support to all families admitted to the ante-partum and NICU units at Baylor All Saints.

Chapter 4

Knowing When to Partner

"Coming together is a beginning, keeping together is progress, working together is success."

~Henry Ford

As an astute social entrepreneur, it would behoove you to consider other alternatives to starting a new nonprofit. There are already approximately a million and a half existing organizations all vying for a share of the shrinking pool of charitable dollars. Partnering with a nonprofit in your community may be the perfect opportunity for your yet-to-be organization. Or, opening a local chapter of an existing nationally chartered nonprofit may be an option worth pursuing. When you consider the stiff competition for charitable contributions, these options may be the safest bet to ensure the viability of your programs and/or services.

Since you've already completed a thorough needs analysis of the services in your community, it should be easier to narrow down the list of nonprofits that offer compatible programs and services that would be complemented by what your organization is interested in offering. If you're considering the pursuit of this option, I would recommend that you target three to five organizations for a potential partnership.

Most nonprofits have excellent websites that provide contact lists for the organization's staff and board members' names. If you know any of the people involved in leading the organization, I would begin by making an appointment to meet with them and to discuss the possibility of combining forces. You will have to negotiate your involvement in this option, so you must be prepared to sacrifice some control if you choose to pursue this alternative.

Joining Forces

During difficult economic times, you will find that many nonprofits have chosen (others have been forced to band together to survive) to think out-of-the-box and may be receptive to creative partnership opportunities. Collaboration can be the perfect solution for organizations with complementary programs and services. On the other hand, a merger may work well in fields with a large number of service providers that are geographically fragmented and asset intensive.

Some well-known organizations are instituting these strategically innovative options, for example:

Merger: The Badger Association of the Blind & Visually Impaired, of Milwaukee, merged with the Center for Blind & Visually Impaired Children. The organization has launched a new identity and the newly formed organization is now known as Vision Forward Association.

Merger: SafeHaven was formed through a merger of Women's Haven and The Women's Shelter. SafeHaven's two emergency shelters, one in Arlington and one in Fort Worth, accommodate a combined 174 women and children, making SafeHaven one of the largest shelters in Texas.

Merger: Girl Scouts of Northeast Texas was born from the merger of the Cross Timbers, Red River Valley, and Texas Girl Scout Councils in Texas.

Merger/Consolidation: The American Red Cross is rearranging its chapters in 2012. The Southwestern Pennsylvania Region will merge with the Northwestern Pennsylvania Region to form the new American Red Cross Western Pennsylvania Region. According to officials, the business decision "is designed to increase local services and disaster-response capacity while making more efficient use of donated dollars."

These organizations are determined to reap the financial benefits of consolidating administrative functions. The expense sharing of back-office operations can provide for increased efficiency, as well as boost the bottom line of strained budgets. Some areas you may want to consider for consolidation include:

* Administrative Management
* Accounting/Human Resources
    * Payroll
    * Benefits
    * Accounts Payable and Accounts Receivable
* Maintenance
* Information Technology

By reducing costs and operating more efficiently, organizations are able to focus on providing services and the fulfillment of their missions. Another way that organizations are improving their bottom line by merging or consolidating is that they are reducing the number of organizations competing for the same donations. The preference of donors varies—some prefer to give to larger national organizations, while others prefer to donate to those delivering services in their community, so keep that in mind when discussing merger possibilities.

Benefits of Partnering

* Increase the overall impact and number of clients served
* Accelerate the successful achievement of the organization's missions
* Address a planned succession of one of the organization's leaders
* Save costs and improve operating efficiencies

As you explore all of your options, you may discover that partnering with an existing organization will be the best way to serve your community. If you are able to connect with the right partner, the benefits of their experience and reputation will far exceed any real or perceived costs.

Part 2
Building the Foundation

Chapter 5

Assembling a Productive Volunteer Board

> "I choose to rise up out of that storm and see that in moments of desperation, fear, and helplessness, each of us can be a rainbow of hope, doing what we can to extend ourselves in kindness and grace to one another. And I know for sure that there is no them, there's only us."
>
> ~Oprah Winfrey, American Icon

Selecting your board of directors will be one of the most critical tasks you will undertake. This group of volunteers will govern your organization and will be ultimately responsible for its success or failure.

You must consider the needs of your particular organization when populating the board. A sample matrix is included at the end of this chapter to provide you with a guide to use in the selection of your prospective members. This matrix will also be helpful when you are considering adding new members in the future. You may choose to change any of the criteria listed, or perhaps add attributes you feel necessary in the selection of qualified and dedicated volunteer board members.

It would be a mistake to not clearly define the roles and responsibilities of your board of directors. The following job description may be helpful for you when defining the responsibilities required by your volunteer board.

Board Member Sample Job Description

As outlined by the bylaws of _____, a nonprofit corporation, the board supports the fulfillment of the organization's mission by providing leadership, strategic governance, and oversight. Specific board member position responsibilities include:

* Serving as an advisor to the nonprofit organization's chief executive in the development and implementation of the strategic plan
* Charged with the review of the organization's overall outcomes and metrics in the evaluation, its impact, and regularly measuring the effectiveness of the organization's programs using those metrics; reviewing board meeting agendas and documents in preparation of board or committee meetings
* Provide the approval of the organization's annual operating budget, external audit reports, fundraising plan, and other business decisions; perform any and all duties imposed either collectively or individually by law, by the Articles of Incorporation or the organization's bylaws
* Participate in the annual performance evaluation of the chief executive, as well as the annual evaluation of the governing body
* Assist the chief executive and board president in the identification and recruitment of new members of the board
* Participate in orienting newly appointed members to the organization, its mission, and strategic plan
* Partner with the chief executive and other board members, ensuring board resolutions are executed
* Volunteer to serve on committees and take on special assignments, as required by the needs of the organization
* Represent the organization as an ambassador in the community
* Fundraising

Board members will make this nonprofit organization a charitable priority, providing annual donations as a reflection of their commitment. The organization expects to have 100% of members "give or get" an annual contribution in the amount of $_____.

(continued)

Board Member Sample Job Description (continued)

Terms and Participation

Board members will serve a _____-year term and will be eligible for re-election for _____ additional term(s). Board meetings will be held _____ and committee meetings will be scheduled as needed to fulfill its particular purpose.

Qualifications

Board service is an exceptional opportunity for individuals passionate about the mission of _____, a nonprofit corporation. The board aims to attract persons with significant executive leadership accomplishments in business, government, philanthropy, or the nonprofit sector. Additionally, members should embody a commitment, understanding, and passion for the organization's clients and stakeholders.

Service on the organization's board of directors is voluntary and members will serve without remuneration.

Mission and Vision

Once assembled, the board's first task will be outlining the new organization's mission and vision. As the "brainchild" of the organization, you will likely have this mapped out already, so the board should review, refine, and officially accept the operating purpose(s) of the organization.

This may come as a surprise to you, but the mission and vision will need to be reviewed annually, at a minimum. As your organization grows and evolves, the mission may need to evolve, as well. The statement should succinctly state the organization's purpose, strategic goals, and the population your organization will serve.

For your perusal, I have included some mission statements from nonprofit organizations. Of course, you have a great deal of latitude when crafting your organization's mission statement, but you should take your time in reviewing and comparing what you find compelling about the following statements:

"The mission of Mothers Against Drunk Driving is to stop drunk driving, support the victims of this violent crime, and prevent underage drinking." Mothers Against Drunk Driving, http://www.madd.org/about-us/mission/.

"The mission of The Nature Conservancy is to preserve the plants, animals, and natural communities that represent the diversity of life on Earth by protecting the lands and waters they need to survive." The Nature Conservancy, http://www.nature.org/aboutus/visionmission/index.htm.

"To inspire hope and contribute to health and well-being by providing the best care to every patient through integrated clinical practice, education, and research." The Mayo Clinic, http://www.mayoclinic.org/about/missionvalues.html.

"To provide effective means for the prevention of cruelty to animals throughout the United States." The American Society for the Prevention of Cruelty to Animals, http://www.aspca.org/About-Us.aspx.

"The increase and diffusion of knowledge." The Smithsonian Institution, http://si.edu/About/Mission.

Although I have a deep and abiding respect for all of the organizations listed above, I am most partial to the Smithsonian's mission statement. I have had the pleasure of serving one of their affiliate organizations and am enamored by the simplicity and brevity of their statement—I doubt that their employees or board members have any difficulty in reciting the mission. Amazingly, the mission statement's conciseness does not diminish the enormity of the 165-year-old organization's mission.

As you will notice, the first two statements use the corporation's name in the mission, while the others don't. This is your preference when crafting your mission statement—remember you have creative license in this regard. Be wary—some board members can get caught up in "wordsmithing" and bring this assignment to a screeching halt. As the founder, you will want to ensure the drafting and subsequent reviews of the mission statement process remains on track. The statement should spell out your organization's purpose in as few words as possible, to quickly grab the public's attention and make a lasting, positive impression.

Chief Executive

Now that the organization's mission statement has been agreed upon, the next primary task for the board of directors to tackle is the selection and subsequent management of the organization's chief executive, often called the Executive Director, President, and/or Chief Executive Officer. As the founder, this may be the position you envision for yourself.

The chief executive is responsible for the day-to-day operations of the organization, while the board of directors is responsible for the governance of the organization. The line between managing and governing can get crossed, so it is important that job descriptions be reviewed often. The board must aid in the creation of the executive's job description and ensure that the person selected for the job is the most qualified candidate to lead the organization.

Once selected, the board must work in harmony with the chief executive and the organization's staff to fulfill the mission and vision. The board is obligated to provide the necessary support for the selected individual and nurture the partnership as in any other employee/employer relationship; providing professional annual evaluations of the executive's progress toward the attainment of the goals prescribed and defined by the board. It is extremely unlikely that an organization will successfully achieve its mission if the board of directors and staff are working in opposition to each other. Many skilled executive directors, dedicated boards, and wonderful organizations have been derailed by unproductive and vengeful board members. It only takes one "bad" board member to poison the entire board and if this individual is well-connected, they can single-handedly destroy the organization's reputation in the community.

It should be clear to volunteers, board members, and employees of your organization that they are individually and collectively responsible for the organization's public image. Every person associated with the organization should strive to enhance the organization's image in the eyes of the public. You and your organization will benefit greatly if you continually report (verbally and in writing) on the successes and forward momentum of the organization. If you reiterate the information you want communicated in the community, you must continually strive to keep the lines of communication open. You will be pleasantly surprised by the results of providing board members with the script you want them to use.

Goals and Fundraising

Effectual planning is another primary step in building a steady foundation by the members of a nonprofit organization's board. The directors should reach a consensus on the goals that the organization will need to meet in order to achieve its mission. In the beginning, your corporation's board should consist of a large percentage of members that are willing to "roll up their sleeves" to get the job done. Especially when your organization is in the infant stage, you will need as many talented volunteers that you can solicit. If the right members are selected, your organization can benefit tremendously from the skills and experience of a diverse board.

Above all other cornerstones of the strong organizational foundation, board members are responsible for the financial viability of the organization. This is a difficult hurdle for many organizations, as you will undoubtedly have members with the capacity to give at different levels and who have a varying number of community and business connections. Just because an individual has the ability to give or willingness to ask their contacts for charitable contributions to your organization, doesn't necessarily mean that they will follow through. Oftentimes, board members will be connected to multiple organizations within the community and will typically give based on their level of commitment and passion for each organization's mission. Disappointingly, you may discover that your organization does not rate at the top of all of your board members' contribution lists. I strongly advise that you have your board members sign an agreement and/or an annual financial commitment, with the expected contribution amount listed.

It is hard for many of us to solicit charitable donations from our family, friends, colleagues, and associates, much less new friends that we meet in the community. While some people are natural-born salespeople, a large number of people will have to hone their "sales" skills. Larger communities may have educational centers designed to support nonprofit organizations and may offer training programs for you, your staff, and board members, including all facets of fundraising. Another option is to enlist the services of a professional fundraiser to guide your organization in the development of an effective fundraising plan. We will explore fundraising plans in Section 5 of this book.

The board of directors is responsible for the overall financial integrity of the organization and for the provision of adequate funds to fulfill the organization's mission and programs. Organizations have different ways of bringing in revenue. These may include program revenues, membership fees, individual giving, corporate sponsorships, government grants, foundation grants, event revenues, an annual fund, and a myriad of social enterprises, like gift shops, movies, space rentals, catering, or even medical clinics. It is important that board members are aware of their personal financial commitment as a board member. For example, if your organization will rely heavily on special events for revenue, board members should enjoy inviting their friends and colleagues to this type of event. It will be you and your board's option as to whether event support will apply to the members' annual commitment.

In my community, several organizations have an annual "give or get" financial responsibility for board members. For example, if the commitment is $5,000, the board member may elect to write a personal or business check for that amount or will solicit charitable donations from their friends and associates. For example, a board member may write a personal check for $1,000 and solicit donations from their contacts for the remaining $4,000. If your organization fits the mold of a typical nonprofit, you will have a percentage of members that will not meet their annual commitment, some that meet the goal, and happily, some members will exceed the established board commitment.

By law, board members are legally responsible for financial oversight and the protection of the organization's assets. The finance committee works hand-in-hand with the staff to develop the annual budget, which is presented to the full board for their approval. When the board Treasurer presents financials during board meetings, the revenues and expenses should be shown in comparison to the board approved budget. Additionally, the Sarbanes-Oxley requirements that apply to nonprofit organizations, require written financial controls be in place. With charitable organizations, the legal, financial, and ethical buck stops with the board of directors. They must ensure that the staff members are qualified and committed to fulfilling all of their job requirements.

As mentioned at the beginning of this chapter, as a leader of a nonprofit organization, you must build an effectual volunteer board of directors. The members must be passionate about your mission; comfortable sharing the mission and soliciting donations from the community-at-large; and be competent to serve in the fulfillment of the mission and their duties.

The particular needs of your organization must be weighed when populating the board of directors. A sample matrix is provided below as a guide in the selection of your prospective members. This matrix will also be helpful when you are considering adding new members in the future. You may choose to add/delete or change any of the criteria listed, which you feel are appropriate in the selection of qualified and dedicated volunteer board members. It may be helpful for you to perform an Internet search for nonprofit board selection matrixes that may be a better fit for your type of organization.

While building your initial board, you will need to decide what size board will be most productive in your organization's circumstances. I strongly recommend that your board not exceed fifteen members. A board of this size provides for a diverse group, as well as a broad basis for support.

Sample Board Selection Matrix

	Current Board Make-Up							Prospective Board Members			
	Member A	Member B	Member C	Member D	Member E	Member F	Member G	Prospect A	Prospect B	Prospect C	Prospect D
Attributes											
Gender											
Age											
Ethnicity/Race											
Geographical area											
Faith											
Political affiliation											
Knowledge/Expertise											
Educational											
Financial											
Human Resources											
Legal											
Marketing											
Technology (IT)											
Government official											
Business development											
Nonprofit board experience											
Core Compentecies											
Visonary/strategic alliances											
Community connections											
Fundraising abilities											
Public speaking											
Leadership											

Chapter 6

What's the Big Deal about Bylaws?

"The best way to find yourself, is to lose yourself in the service of others."

~Ghandi

The bylaws will serve as your organization's official operating policies and procedures manual. Bylaws must clearly define:

* Size of the board and how it will function
* Roles and duties of directors and officers
* Rules and procedures for holding meetings, electing directors, and appointing officers
* Other essential corporate governance matters, including the role of board committees

Your state's laws governing charitable organizations typically address non-profit governance matters. Of course, you may choose different rules, as long as they aren't in violation of state law and are specifically included in your bylaws. If you choose to follow state law, restating them in your bylaws ensures that all your operating rules are in one document.

Your organization's bylaws are not required to be open to public inspection, but you should consider making them readily available to promote transparency and encourage your board of directors to pay close attention to them. Your bylaws should be reviewed regularly by the board of directors and amended as the organization grows and evolves.

Recently, nonprofit trends have leaned toward more relaxed wording in organizational bylaws. It has been my experience that it is extremely important to have detailed expectations for directors' conduct and requirements. It is quite common for nonprofit boards to have to reign in one of their fellow directors. Typically, nonprofit boards are populated by driven, successful business and community leaders that may not be accustomed to working as a team member with their peers. The possible challenges may range from bullying and confrontational behavior to a general lack of interest and poor attendance.

No matter the particular situation, it will be difficult to confront underperforming or misbehaving board members. Having strong bylaws will provide an excellent basis for the conversation with the board member and will provide a written document of what the organization requires from the governing body.

If your state requires exempt organizations to file annual returns, you must report name, address, and structural and operational changes to your bylaws on the return. Some states may also require you to file bylaws and report changes.

Please be aware that bylaws are very specific for each organization, so you will want to change them to meet your nonprofit organization's needs.

For your convenience, a sample copy of bylaws is provided below:

BYLAWS OF
OF

_____

A Nonprofit Corporation

ARTICLE I — OFFICES

Section 1 — Name: The principal office of the Corporation shall be located in the City of _____, County of _____, within the State of _____. The Corporation may also maintain offices at such other places as the board of directors may, from time to time, determine.

ARTICLE II — PURPOSE

Section 1 — Internal Revenue Code, Section 501(c)(3) Purpose: Said Corporation is organized exclusively for charitable, religious, educational, or scientific purposes, including for such purposed, the making of distributions to organizations that qualify as exempt organizations under section 501(c)(3) of the Internal Revenue Code, or the corresponding section of any future tax code. The specific purpose of the Corporation is:

_____
_____
_____
_____
_____
_____.

Section 2 — No private inurement: No part of the net earnings of the corporation shall inure to the benefit of or be distributable to its members, trustees, officers, or other private persons, except that of the Corporation shall be authorized and empowered to pay reasonable compensation for services rendered and to make payments and distributions in furtherance of the purposes set forth in Section 1 hereof.

(continued)

BYLAWS *(continued)*

Section 3 — No lobbying activities: No substantial part of the activities of the Corporation shall be the carrying on of propaganda, or otherwise attempting to influence legislation, and the Corporation shall not participate in, or intervene in any political campaign on behalf of or in opposition to any candidate for public office. Notwithstanding any other provision of these articles, this Corporation shall not engage in any activities or exercise any powers that are not in furtherance of the purposes of the Corporation.

ARTILE III - DIRECTORS

Section 1 — Number: The number of initial directors (members) of this corporation shall be _____ and collectively, they will be known as the board of directors. This number can be increased/decreased by the amendment of these bylaws by the board, but shall in no case be fewer than _____ director(s).

Section 2 — Duties: It shall be the duty of the Corporation's directors to:

• Perform any and all duties imposed on them either collectively or individually by law, by the Articles of Incorporation, or by these bylaws;

• Appoint and remove, employ and discharge, and except as otherwise provided in these bylaws, prescribe the duties and determine the compensation of all officers, agents, and employees of the corporation;

• Supervise all officers, agents, and employees of the corporation to ensure that their duties are performed satisfactorily and efficiently;

• Meet at such times and places as required by these bylaws; and

• Register their addresses with the Secretary of the board of the corporation and notices of meetings delivered to them at such address shall be valid.

Section 3 — Terms: Board members shall serve ____-year terms, but are eligible for re-election for up to _____ consecutive terms.

Section 4 — Resignation, termination, and absences: Any officer may resign at any time by providing written notice to the Corporation's board Chair

(continued)

BYLAWS *(continued)*

and/or board Secretary. Such resignation shall take effect immediately upon certification of the Secretary. Board members may be terminated from the board due to excessive absences, without prior approval. A board member may be removed, with or without cause, by a majority vote of the remaining directors.

Section 5 — Vacancies: When a vacancy on the board arises, the Secretary or Chair of the nominating committee must receive nominations for new members from present board members in advance of a scheduled board meeting. The nominations, along with the nominees' resumes, shall be sent out to board members with the regular board-meeting announcement, to be voted upon at the next board meeting.

Section 6 — Meetings and notice: The board shall meet _____ (times per year), at an agreed-upon time and place. An official board meeting requires that each board member have written notice in advance.

Section 7 — Special meetings: Special meetings of the board shall be called upon the request of the Chair, or one-third of the board. Notices of special meetings shall be sent out by the Secretary to each board member at least two weeks in advance.

Section 8 — Quorum for meetings: A quorum for the Corporation's board of directors shall require _____% of the members of the board of directors.

Except as otherwise provided under the Articles of Incorporation, these bylaws, or provision of law, no business shall be considered by the board at any meeting at which the required quorum is not present and the only motion the chair shall entertain is the motion to adjourn.

Section 9 — Election procedures: New directors shall be elected by a majority of directors present at such a meeting, provided there is a quorum present. Directors so elected shall serve a term beginning _____.

(continued)

BYLAWS *(continued)*

Section 10 — Officers and duties: There shall be a minimum of four officers of the board, consisting of a Chair, Vice-Chair, Secretary, and Treasurer. Their duties are as follows:

The *Chair* shall convene regularly scheduled board meetings, shall preside or arrange for other members of the Executive Committee to preside at each meeting in the following order: Vice-chair, Secretary, and then Treasurer.

The *Vice-Chair* shall chair committees on special subjects as designated by the board.

The *Secretary* shall be responsible for keeping records of board actions, including overseeing the taking of minutes at all board meetings, sending out meeting announcements, distributing copies of minutes and the agenda to each board member, and assuring that corporate records are properly maintained.

The *Treasurer* shall make a report at each board meeting. The Treasurer shall chair the finance committee and ensure accurate financial information is available to board members and the public.

ARTICLE IV — COMMITTEES

Section 1 — Committee formation: The board may create committees as needed, such as fundraising, governance, programming, public relations/marketing, audit, etc. The board Chair appoints all Committee Chairs.

Section 2 — Executive Committee: The four officers serve as the members of the Executive Committee. Except for the power to amend the Articles of Incorporation and bylaws, the Executive Committee shall have all the powers and authority of the board of directors in the intervals between meetings of the board of directors, and is subject to the direction and control of the full board.

(continued)

BYLAWS *(continued)*

Section 3 — Finance Committee: The Treasurer is the chair of the Finance Committee, which should include at least three other independent members. The Finance Committee is responsible for developing and reviewing fiscal procedures and the annual budget with staff and other board members. The board must approve the budget and all expenditures must be within budget. Any major change in the budget must be approved by the board or the Executive Committee. The fiscal year shall be _____. Annual reports are required to be submitted to the board showing income, expenditures, and pending income. The financial records of the organization are public information and shall be made available to the members, board members, and the public-at-large.

ARTICLE V — AMENDMENTS

Section 1 — Amendments: These bylaws may be amended when necessary by a majority vote of the board of directors. Proposed amendments must be submitted to the Secretary and included with regular board announcements.

ARTICLE VI — INDEMNIFICATION

Section 1 — Indemnification: Any officer, director, or employee of the Corporation shall be indemnified and held harmless to the full extent allowed by law.

Section 2 — Insurance: The Corporation shall obtain insurance providing for indemnification of directors, officers, and employees.

The bylaws of the Corporation have been adopted and certified by the board of directors on _____.

Secretary_____

Date   _____

A Closer Look at Board Governance

What is board governance? A common definition of governance is *the act or manner of governing; to sway or persuade*. This is concisely the role of your board's governance committee.

After assembling a dedicated and astute board of directors, it is important that the governing body have a strategic roadmap, along with the requisite authority to operate in the most efficient and productive manner possible. The role of the governance committee is to review and revise, develop and draft, and oversee policies and practices of the board of directors and staff. The governance practices of the nonprofit organization will address matters of transparency, board members' independence, accountability, fiduciary responsibilities, and oversight of the organization's chief executive. Additionally, the governance committee will design and review the composition of the board of directors, making recommendations and the continual re-evaluation of the requirements and the subsequent identification of new members.

Sample Governance Committee Charter

This Governance Committee Charter has been adopted by the board of directors of _____, a nonprofit corporation, on _____.

Purpose

Pursuant to the organization's bylaws, the purpose of the governance committee is to:

- Keep the board of directors informed of corporate best practices
- Continually review and revise (if necessary), the committee's governance practices
- Offer advice to those charged with the selection and appointment of new directors as to the skill-set needs, background, and professional or educational experiences necessary for effectual board service

(continued)

Sample Governance Committee Charter *(continued)*

Powers of the Governance Committee

The organization's board authorizes the governance committee to use the power and authority necessary to:

- Obtain required information from the executive staff of the organization;
- Seek and obtain advice and assistance from legal or accounting professionals, as the committee or board of directors deems necessary; and
- Negotiate any financial contracts associated with professional contractors and present them to the full board for approval prior to any contract's execution.

Committee Selection

The committee shall be populated by members appointed by the organization's board of directors. The board chair shall select and name the committee's chair. The members shall serve until their term or service is terminated or until such time their successors shall be selected and appointed. The committee will ensure the seamless transition by planning for the succession of the committee's chair.

Committee members should be independent, refraining from engaging in any private business transactions or receiving any compensation from the organization or related entities.

Governance committee members shall be knowledgeable in matters relating to corporate governance, especially as related to nonprofit organizations.

Meetings

The committee shall meet a minimum of _____ times per year. Additional meetings may be required for the productive and successful operation of the board of directors and its related organization.

Meeting agendas will be prepared in advance of the meeting and minutes of the meeting will be recorded.

(continued)

Sample Governance Committee Charter *(continued)*

Reports

The committee shall:

- Provide a written report of the committee's actions and make recommendations at the board's next scheduled meeting;
- Provide a committee assessment and propose any changes to this charter as part of the annual self-evaluation of the board of directors; and
- Act with the unanimous consent of the committee.

Evaluation Responsibilities

The governance committee should undertake the continual review, revision, or development of the organization's written policies regarding conflicts of interest and whistleblower protection. Such policies should conform and satisfy any applicable laws and regulations for nonprofit corporations. Furthermore, the organizational bylaws, committee structure and charters, as well as other governance documents should be reviewed, updated, and/or modified (if necessary) on an annual basis. In addition, the governance committee should regularly review the organization's policies and procedures guiding hiring, compensation, and employment practices.

As mentioned at the beginning of this chapter, state laws governing charitable organizations usually address nonprofit governance affairs. If you choose to use different rules, ensure that they aren't in violation of the state laws.

Chapter 7

Board Agreements, Training, and Meetings

"The test of our worth is the service we render."

~Theodore Roosevelt, U.S. President

Just as the bylaws provide for your organization's official operating policies and procedures manual, you will need to outline what is expected of board members and how their participation will benefit the corporation.

One way to plainly spell out this information is to institute a board member "contract." This is not intended to be a legally enforceable document, but rather a well-defined agreement.

Sample Board Member Agreement

I, _____, understand that as a member of the board of directors of _____, I have a fiduciary, legal, and ethical responsibility to ensure the success of the organization. I believe in the purpose and the mission of the organization, and I will act responsibly and prudently as its steward. As part of my responsibilities as a board member, I will:

- Interpret the organization's programmatic outcomes and values to the community, represent the organization, and act as an ambassador.

- Interpret our stakeholders' needs and values to the organization; speak out for their interests; and on their behalf, hold the organization accountable.

- Attend at least 75% of board meetings, committee meetings, and special events.

- Reach my personal financial contribution commitment by personal donation or the solicitation of my contacts.

- Actively participate in one or more fundraising activities.

- Notify the board chair and excuse myself from discussions and votes where I have a potential conflict of interest.

- Stay informed about what's going on in the organization, asking questions and requesting information.

- Actively participate in and take responsibility for making decisions on issues, policies, and other matters.

- Work in good faith with staff and other board members as partners toward achievement of the organization's goals.

If I am not fulfilling these commitments to the organization, I expect the board chair will call me to discuss these responsibilities.

(continued)

Sample Board Member Agreement *(continued)*

Organization Responsibility

In turn, the organization will be responsible to me in the following ways:

- I will be sent, without having to request them, quarterly financial reports and an update of organizational activities that will allow me to meet the "prudent person" standards of the law. (The "prudent person rule" states that an individual must act with similar judgment and care as a prudent person would act, in a like situation.)

- Opportunities will be offered to me to discuss the organization's programs, goals, activities, and status of such with the chief executive and board chair.

- The organization will assist me in the performance of my duties by keeping me informed about issues in the industry and field in which we are working and by offering me opportunities for professional development as a board member.

- Board members and staff will respond in a timely and straightforward fashion to questions that I feel are necessary for me to carry out my fiscal, legal, and ethical responsibilities to the nonprofit organization. Board members and staff will work in good faith with me toward achievement of our mutual goals.

If the organization is not fulfilling its obligation to me, I can call on the board chair and/or chief executive to discuss the organization's obligations.

Signed_____, Board Member
Date _____

Signed_____, Board Chair
Date_____

The board chair should sign two copies of this agreement for each board member. New board members should sign both copies, return one copy to the secretary of the board, and keep the other for their personal reference. Signing the agreements ensures that board members will read them, and signifies the importance of the contract.

Do not miss your best opportunity to introduce your incoming board members to your organization, your mission, and staff during a board orientation session. This will be the perfect opportunity for board members to meet each other. A thorough and in-depth manual will be an excellent tool for new members to use throughout their board service with your organization. The manual should be prepared with care and provide an overview of all of the operations and programming.

The following is a recommended list of items that should be included in your Board Orientation manual:

The board

* A current list of board members, along with their professional bios
* Board member job description and statement of responsibilities

Background of organization

* Brief history
* Articles of Incorporation
* Bylaws
* IRS determination letter

Strategic framework

* Mission and vision statement
* Strategic plan

Board policies and procedures

* Conflicts of interest policy
* Whistleblower policy
* Directors and officers insurance policy information

Finance and fundraising

* Most recent annual report and audit report
* Current annual budget
* Form 990
* Banking resolutions
* Investment policy
* Current funder list

Staff

* A current staff list with extensions and email addresses
* Organizational chart

Marketing and Promotional Materials

* Annual calendar
* Website information
* Membership brochure, information brochure, program materials

Board Orientation

New board members will need an introduction to your organization, the mission, the programs, the staff members, as well as their fellow board members and the organizational rules and regulations, and, naturally, what his/her job involves. You will want the orientation for board members to be similar to that of your staff members.

Remember—your board members will not only be donors, but will also be soliciting contributions from their friends and associates. Therefore, you will want to provide a comprehensive and well-thought-out manual.

Recipe for Success

Successful training sessions require structure, training materials, knowledgeable trainers, and receptive board appointees that are anxious and willing to assume their important roles. For board member orientation, these ingredients consist of the following:

* Structure: Timing, sessions, materials
* Training materials: Orientation manual, legal and organizational supporting documents
* Trainers: Member of the governance committee, board chair, chief executive and/or key staff members
* Board members: New appointees and present members to serve as ambassadors and mentors for the new members

Ongoing Orientation

Board member orientation is an ongoing event, scheduled as needed throughout the year. The process starts during the initial cultivation meeting and continues through the member's participation in their first board meeting. When recruiting new members, you will provide an introduction to the organization, explain why you are involved in the organization, why you think the recruit would be a good fit for the board, and discuss the merits of board service. Initial orientation sessions are scheduled as new members are appointed and will cover all pertinent information new members will need to properly serve the organization.

Training Materials

Each new board member should receive an organized and thorough board book. This manual will serve as a permanent reference tool, including background information and legal and financial documents that are critical for board work. Some organizations provide the manual in an electronic format, while others will provide a hardcopy manual. A board manual should be kept current and include at least the following documents:

* List of all board members, their terms, and their contact information; a short biography of the chief executive (a couple of paragraphs); and an organizational chart
* Board member agreement, job descriptions of the officers, all committee charters, and a list of members

* Articles of Incorporation, bylaws, most recent IRS Form 990, board-related policies, directors, and officers insurance information
* A short organizational history, including a timeline of key historical events, mission statement, and fact sheet about the industry.

Trainers

Since orientation will be a formal part of your board education, your governance committee is responsible for new member recruitment, as well as helping your board members perform at their best. The governance committee will aid in the planning of the orientation process.

The board chair should be involved in orienting new board members. The chair has the ability to excite and motivate new members, and brings clarity to her/his role and authority. Because the chief executive knows the organization best, the executive is the most appropriate person to provide the organization's background and purpose. This is a perfect opportunity for new members to observe the chief executive in action and begin building a working relationship. When appropriate, outside experts may be asked to facilitate a part of the session to talk about relevant industry issues, legal matters, or other subjects to help new members get a better grasp of their responsibilities.

Mentors

New board members may be assigned a current member of the board as a mentor. A peer is perfectly suited to answer detailed questions that might surface during orientation or board meetings. When a new member needs additional background information, the mentor can provide expert direction concerning the board, the staff, and the organization.

Orientation is an exceptional opportunity for board members to get to know one other and to begin building camaraderie. The small group, in-depth business discussion about the organization will help members feel comfortable and prepared for participation in the next board meeting.

Continuing Education

The governance committee, the board chair, and the chief executive should ensure that the board embeds learning opportunities into routine governance work, as well. Many organizations include learning opportunities in the annual board retreat.

The opportunities for training should be designed for the specific needs of your organization and governing body. For example, if you have a high percentage of directors that are new to board service, you may ask an expert in board issues to speak during your annual meeting. Check to see if you have a nonprofit educational organization in your area. In my large metropolitan community, we have the Center for Nonprofit Management in Dallas, as well as the Funding Information Center in Fort Worth. Both of these organizations provide advice and educational opportunities for nonprofit employees, volunteers, and especially board members. They offer programs at their facilities and will often coordinate training programs at your site. These services are typically provided at a great rate for member organizations.

The possibilities for training opportunities are numerous. If your organization is launching a new capital campaign, you may provide a session on how to solicit large donations. Another option if your organization provides social services is to have an expert in the field talk with your board members about the latest trends. If your organization serves the homeless population, the training could provide information about recent research findings, updates on funding opportunities, and results of successful programs.

Board Meeting Agenda and Minutes

Productive and efficient meetings begin with a concise agenda. The agenda should include all business that you anticipate will be discussed. It is a good idea to check with the other organizers to see if any new business should be added to the agenda. Most of your routine board meetings will follow the same order and structure and a basic outline is shown next.

Agenda
Meeting of the Board of Directors
of
(Name of Organization)
(Date and Time of Meeting)

I. Call to Order   President

II. Approval of the Minutes   Secretary

Prior Board Meeting (include the date of the meeting)

III. Reports of Officers and Committees   Committee Chairs

   A. Treasurer's Report   Treasurer

Financial results from the previous period
   • Comparison of actual results to budget

   B. Governance Committee Report   Governance Chair

Nomination of any new members

IV. New Business   All

Organizational calendar

V. Adjourn   President

Minutes

Minutes (a synopsis of the meeting details) should be recorded at each meeting of the board of directors and any established committees. The minutes should include the name of your organization and the date and time of the meeting should also be noted. Next, list the names of those members present at the meeting, and then names of the absent members. The names of the staff members in attendance should also be indicated in the minutes of the meeting.

Part 3

Getting and Staying Legal

Chapter 8

Applying for Incorporation

"Though government has an important role to play in meeting the many challenges that remain before us, we are coming to understand that no organization, including government, will fully succeed without the active participation of each of us. Volunteers are vital to enabling this country to live up to the true promise of its heritage."

~Bill Clinton, U.S. President

The time has arrived for you to begin the application process. If you've done your homework, this should be a breeze. Thus far, you've done a thorough environmental scan; perfected your mission and vision; assembled your initial board of directors; and you've prepared your bylaws.

Let's take a closer look at developing your Articles of Incorporation. Many states provide fill-in-the-blank forms for your use, but you will want to make sure that the articles appropriately reflect your intentions for your organization's structure and purpose. Here is a sample to give you a "jumping off" point to begin your development process.

Sample Articles of Incorporation

ARTICLES OF INCORPORATION
OF

_____

A Nonprofit Corporation

Pursuant to the provision of the Nonprofit Corporation Act of this state, the undersigned incorporator(s) adopt the following Articles of Incorporation to form a nonprofit corporation.

ARTICLE I — NAME, PURPOSE, AND DURATION

Section 1 — Name: The name of the organization shall be _____. It shall be a nonprofit organization incorporated under the laws of the state of _____.

The name and address of the registered agent and registered offices of this corporation are:

_____

_____

_____

_____

_____.

Section 2 — Purpose: The purposes for which **[Insert name of nonprofit]** is organized are for the following charitable, scientific, or educational purposes:

_____

_____

_____

_____

_____.

(continued)

ARTICLES OF INCORPORATION *(continued)*

Section 3 — Duration: The period of the duration of this corporation is:

_____ .

Section 4 — Dissolution: Upon the dissolution of the corporation, assets shall be distributed for one or more exempt purposes within the meaning of section 501(c)(3) of the Internal Revenue Code, or the corresponding section of any future federal tax code, or shall be distributed to the federal government, or to a state or local government, for a public purpose. Any such assets not so disposed shall be disposed of by a Court of Competent Jurisdiction of the county in which the principal office of the corporation is then located, exclusively for such purposes or to such organizations, as said Court shall determine, which are operated exclusively for such purposes.

ARTICLE II — BOARD OF DIRECTORS

Section 1 — Membership: The number of initial directors (members) of this corporation shall be _____ and their names and addresses are:

_____

_____

_____

_____ .

Section 2 — Board role and size: The board is responsible for overall policy and direction of the organization, and formally entrusts the responsibility of day-to-day operations to the Executive Director and staff.

Section 3 — Compensation: No part of the net earnings of the corporation shall inure to the benefit of or be distributable to its members, trustees, officers, or other private persons, except that of the corporation shall be authorized and empowered to pay reasonable compensation for services rendered and to make payments and distributions in furtherance of the purposes set forth in Article I, Section 2 hereof. No substantial part of the activities of the corporation shall be the carrying on of propaganda, or otherwise attempting to influence legislation, and the corporation shall not participate in, or intervene in any political campaign on behalf of or in opposition to any candidate for public office. Notwithstanding any other

(continued)

ARTICLES OF INCORPORATION *(continued)*

provision of these articles, this corporation shall not except to an insubstantial degree, engage in any activities or exercise any powers that are not in furtherance of the purposes of the corporation. In as such, board members will serve as volunteers, without compensation other than the reimbursement of reasonable expenses related to their service to the organization.

Section 4 — Terms: All board members shall serve _____-year terms, but are eligible for re-election for up to _____ consecutive terms.

Section 5 — Meetings and notice: The board shall meet _____, at an agreed-upon time and place. An official board meeting requires that each board member have written notice at least two weeks in advance.

Section 6 — Board elections: During the last meeting of each fiscal year of the corporation, the board of directors shall elect directors to replace those whose terms will expire at the end of the fiscal year. This election shall take place during a regular meeting of the directors, called in accordance with the provisions of these bylaws.

Section 7 — Election procedures: New directors shall be elected by a majority of directors present at such a meeting, provided there is a quorum present. Directors so elected shall serve a term beginning

_____.

Section 8 — Quorum: A quorum must be attended by at least _____ percent of board members for business transactions to take place and motions to pass.

Section 9 — Officers and duties: There shall be a minimum of four officers of the board, consisting of a Chair, Vice-chair, Secretary, and Treasurer. Their duties are as follows:

> The *Chair* shall convene regularly scheduled board meetings, shall preside or arrange for other members of the Executive Committee to preside at each meeting in the following order: Vice-chair, Secretary, and then Treasurer.

(continued)

ARTICLES OF INCORPORATION *(continued)*

The *Vice-chair* shall chair committees on special subjects as designated by the board.

The *Secretary* shall be responsible for keeping records of board actions, including overseeing the taking of minutes at all board meetings, sending out meeting announcements, distributing copies of minutes and the agenda to each board member, and assuring that corporate records are maintained.

The *Treasurer* shall make a report at each board meeting. The Treasurer shall chair the finance committee and ensure accurate financial information is available to board members and the public.

Section 10 — Vacancies: When a vacancy on the board arises, the Secretary or Chair of the nominating committee must receive nominations for new members from present board members in advance of a scheduled board meeting. The nominations, along with the nominees' resumes, shall be sent out to board members with the regular board-meeting announcement, to be voted upon at the next board meeting.

Section 11 — Resignation, termination, and absences: Resignation from the board should be in writing and certified by the Secretary. Board members may be terminated from the board due to excessive absences, without prior approval. A board member may be removed for other reasons by a majority vote of the remaining directors.

Section 12 — Special meetings: Special meetings of the board shall be called upon the request of the Chair, or one-third of the board. Notices of special meetings shall be sent out by the Secretary to each board member at least two weeks in advance.

ARTICLE III — COMMITTEES

Section 1 — Committee formation: The board may create committees as needed, such as fundraising, programming, public relations/marketing, audit, etc. The board Chair appoints all Committee Chairs.

(continued)

ARTICLES OF INCORPORATION *(continued)*

Section 2 — Executive Committee: The four officers serve as the members of the Executive Committee. Except for the power to amend the Articles of Incorporation and bylaws, the Executive Committee shall have all the powers and authority of the board of directors in the intervals between meetings of the board of directors, and is subject to the direction and control of the full board.

Section 3 — Finance Committee: The Treasurer is the chair of the Finance Committee, which includes three other board members. The Finance Committee is responsible for developing and reviewing fiscal procedures and the annual budget with staff and other board members. The board must approve the budget and all expenditures must be within budget. Any major change in the budget must be approved by the board or the Executive Committee. The fiscal year shall be _____. Annual reports are required to be submitted to the board showing income, expenditures, and pending income. The financial records of the organization are public information and shall be made available to the members, board members, as well as the public-at-large.

ARTICLE IV — EXECUTIVE DIRECTOR AND STAFF

Section 1 — Executive Director: The Executive Director is selected and hired by the board. The Executive Director has day-to-day responsibilities for the organization, including the fulfillment of the organization's strategic plan. The Executive Director will attend all board meetings, reporting on the progress of the organization. The board may designate other duties as necessary.

ARTICLE V — AMENDMENTS

Section 1 — Amendments: These bylaws may be amended when necessary by a majority vote of the board of directors. Proposed amendments must be submitted to the Secretary and included with regular board announcements.

(continued)

ARTICLES OF INCORPORATION *(continued)*

CERTIFICATION

These undersigned incorporator(s) hereby declare under penalty of perjury that the statements made in the foregoing Articles of Incorporation are true. Furthermore, these bylaws were approved by the board of directors on _____.

Incorporator_____
Date _____

Incorporator_____
Date _____

Incorporator_____
Date _____

As you will notice in the sample articles above, article 1 includes the name of your new organization. In the last section of this book, you will find the contact information for your state to check and reserve the organization's name. Some states require the use of the word corporation or incorporated. Often, the process of checking to see if your chosen name is available and the reservation of the name can be executed online. Be prepared to pay a small fee for this service. You may choose (not required) to trademark your name for protection from others' use in the future. For more information, go to the Patent and Trademark Office's website at www.uspto.gov.

Also in article one; you will state the organization's purpose. Ensure the wording you craft is in line with the Internal Revenue Service's guidelines for exempt purposes. The language required must state that your organization is "organized exclusively for charitable, religious, educational, and scientific purposes, including, for such purposes, the making of distributions to organizations that qualify as exempt organizations under section 501 (c) (3) of the Internal Revenue Code, or corresponding section of any future federal tax code."

Typically, nonprofit organizations complete the blank expected duration or period of time as "perpetuity," since you most likely intend for the organization to serve the community for a period of time with no end.

Article 1, section 4 states what will happen to your organization's assets if you end up dissolving the organization. Of course, you don't plan for this to happen, but it remains a possibility with any organization. The IRS states, "assets shall be distributed for one or more exempt purposes within the meaning of section 501 (c) (3) of the Internal Revenue Code, or corresponding section of any future federal tax code, or shall be distributed to the federal government, or to a state or local government, for the public purpose. Any such assets not disposed of shall be disposed of by the Court of Common Pleas of the county in which the principle office of the organization is then located, exclusively for the purposes or to such organization or organizations, as said court shall determine, which are organized and operated exclusively for such purposes." You do not have to include this exact wording, but you should be clear about your intentions and ensure that the IRS will approve.

Article two spells out the number of initial directors. State laws dictate the minimum number of incorporators (the person(s) that signs the initial documents), as well as the minimum number of directors. The following chart outlines the minimum requirements by state. Because these requirements are subject to change, please verify this information before submitting your final documents.

State	Number of Required Incorporators	Number of Required Directors
Required number of incorporators and directors by state:		
Alabama	1	3
Alaska	3	3
Arizona	1	1
Arkansas	1	3
California	1	1
Colorado	1	1
Connecticut	1	3
Delaware	1	1
District of Columbia	3	3
Florida	1	3
Georgia	1	1
Hawaii	1	3
Idaho	1	3*
Illinois	1	3
Indiana	1	3
Iowa	1	1
Kansas	1	1
Kentucky	1	3
Louisiana	1	3**
Maine	1	3
Maryland	1	1
Massachusetts	1	1
Michigan	1	3

State	Number of Required Incorporators	Number of Required Directors
Minnesota	1	3
Mississippi	1	1
Missouri	1	3
Montana	1	3
Nebraska	1	3
Nevada	1	1
New Hampshire	5	5
New Jersey	1	3
New Mexico	1	3
New York	1	3
North Carolina	1	1
North Dakota	1	3***
Ohio	1	3**
Oklahoma	3	1
Oregon	1	3****
Pennsylvania	1	1
Rhode Island	1	3
South Carolina	1	3
South Dakota	3	3
Tennessee	1	3
Texas	1	3
Utah	1	3
Vermont	1	3
Virginia	1	1

State	Number of Required Incorporators	Number of Required Directors
Washington	1	1
West Virginia	1	3
Wisconsin	1	3
Wyoming	1	3

*Idaho: A minimum of 3 directors is required; religious corporations are permitted to have one director.

**Louisiana and Ohio: A minimum of 3 directors is required, although membership corporations that have fewer than 3 members may have the same number of directors.

***North Dakota: A minimum of 3 directors is required, or at least the numbers of voting members if fewer than 3 voting members exist.

****Oregon: A minimum of 3 directors is required for public benefit corporations. Corporations of religious or mutual benefit are permitted to have one director.

In the sample provided above, the bulk of the remaining articles outline your board's structure, officers, and committees. Again, this is just a sample and should be evaluated and edited to reflect how your organization will be structured. You may revise your bylaws and Articles of Incorporation in the future, but it is easiest to draw up a version that is representative of your vision and that will last for years.

Once your Articles of Incorporation are complete and accepted by your board of directors, you will file for incorporation in the state in which your organization will operate. The contact information is included in the last section of the book. Your state's Secretary of State's office is the agency that will process your name reservation and incorporation. There is a separate fee for each service, which varies by state.

Completing the IRS Forms

The next step for your blossoming nonprofit is to apply for an Employer Identification Number. A copy of IRS Form SS-4, along with the instructions, is provided in the last section. There are several ways to obtain your EIN, including mail, phone, or fax:

EIN Operations

Cincinnati, OH 45999

Phone: (800) 829-4933

FAX: (859) 669-5760

http://www.irs.gov/pub/irs-pdf/fss4.pdf

And now, you're ready to complete the required IRS forms to obtain tax-exempt status. For most nonprofit organizations, you will need to complete IRS Form 1023. This form is available for completion or printing on the IRS's website (http://www.irs.gov/pub/irs-pdf/f1023.pdf) and a copy is also provided in the last section of this book. I would recommend that you use the copy in the back of the book to make notes and fill in information that you will later transfer to the electronic copy.

The Internal Revenue Service also has a publication available to give you some helpful information. Publication 557, *Tax Exempt Status for Your Organization*, the line-by-line instructions for Form 1023, and this book are all useful reference guides to answer most of your outstanding questions.

You are required to file Form 1023 within 27 months from the time your organization filed its Articles of Incorporation (this is the formal date of formation). If the request for tax-exemption is approved, the corporation will be deemed to have been tax-exempt from the beginning. Therefore, any donations received will be treated as such (tax-deductible) for the donors. Although this is permissible, I would recommend that you file for exemption from the beginning. I'm all about taking the least stressful route possible.

For several years now, the IRS has planned to release a software program, Cyber Assistant. When this service becomes available, you will be able to file the required documents completely online for a substantially reduced fee. The latest bulletin that addresses Cyber Assistant (IRS Bulletin 2011-1, dated January 3, 2011) states that the IRS did not anticipate the service would be up and running in 2011. My research did not reveal an official date that Cyber Assistant is expected to be unveiled. Fingers crossed that some of you will be able to take advantage of the new service and save some of the dollars required upfront.

The IRS makes a valiant effort to aid filers of Form 1023. By no means does this make the process any less daunting. Much of the first parts will be easy for you to fill in the requested information because of the hard work you and your board has done so far.

The first page of the packet for Form 1023 contains the following information relating to Part IX:

> *Changes to Parts IX and X are necessary to comply with new regulations that eliminated the advance ruling process. Until Form 1023 is revised to reflect this change, please follow the directions on this notice when completing Part IX and Part X of Form 1023. For more information about the elimination of the advance ruling process, visit us at IRS.gov and click on "Charities and Non-Profits," then in the top right "Search" box type "Elimination of the Advance Ruling Process" (exactly as written) and select "Search."*

Form 1023, Part IX: Financial Data. The instructions at the top of Part IX on page 9 of Form 1023 are now as follows. For purposes of this schedule, years in existence refer to completed tax years.

✳ If in existence less than 5 years, complete the statement for each year in existence and provide projections of your likely revenues and expenses based on a reasonable and good faith estimate of your future finances for a total of:

  • Three years of financial information if you have not completed one tax year, or

  • Four years of financial information if you have completed one tax year.

✳ If in existence 5 or more years, complete the schedule for the most recent 5 tax years. You will need to provide a separate statement that includes information about the most recent 5 tax years because the data table in Part IX has not been updated to provide for a 5th year.

The financial documents you will need to prepare include a budget, a profit and loss statement, and a balance sheet. These forms will be needed not only for the IRS, but may also be required by funding sources you intend to approach for donations. Chapter 13 will discuss these financial documents in greater detail.

❋ Budget: It will be a great planning tool for you, your staff, and board to put together a budget projection. Your first year should be in great detail with supporting documents to back up your assumptions. The next two years (three years total as required by the new IRS rules) may be less detailed. You should use reasonable and conservative data for the anticipated growth of your organization. It is a good policy to *under promise* and *over deliver.* Your budget should reflect the same categories that appear on your profit and loss statement.

❋ Statement of Revenues and Expenses (commonly referred to as a Profit and Loss Statement): Form 1023 — Part IX, Section A:

- Revenues—As indicated on the form, your revenues will be categorized as follows:
    - Gifts, grants, and contributions
    - Membership fees
    - Gross investment income
    - Net unrelated business income
    - Taxes levied for your benefit
    - Value of services or facilities furnished by a governmental agency without charge (in-kind donations)
    - Any other revenue (not listed above or in the following categories)
    - Gross receipts from admissions, merchandise sold, or services performed, or furnishing of facilities in any activity that is related to your exempt purposes
    - Net gain or loss from the sale of capital assets
    - Unusual grants
- Expenses—As indicated on the form, your expenses will be categorized as follows:
    - Fundraising expenses

- Contributions, gifts, grants, or similar amounts paid by your organization
- Member benefits—disbursements to or for the benefit of members
- Compensation of officers, directors, and trustees
- Other salaries and wages
- Interest expense
- Occupancy (includes rent, utilities, etc.)
- Professional fees (legal, accounting, etc.)
- Any other uncategorized expenses (e.g., program services)
- Depreciation and depletion (remember this does not affect your cash position)

* Balance Sheet: Form 1023 — Part IX, Section B: Your balance sheet will reflect your current and anticipated assets and liabilities. The form uses the following categories:

  - Assets
    - Cash
    - Accounts receivable
    - Inventories
    - Bonds and notes receivable
    - Corporate stocks
    - Loans receivable
    - Other investments
    - Depreciable and depletable assets
    - Land
    - Any other assets

  - Liabilities
    - Accounts payable
    - Contributions, gifts, and grants payable
    - Mortgages and notes payable
    - Other liabilities

The net of your assets and liabilities is called your net assets or fund balances—the amount by which your assets exceed your liabilities. Some (or many) of the categories the IRS has chosen to reflect on Form 1023 may not apply to your organization, either at this point or even in the future. Do not be disillusioned if you do not use all of the categories on the form. For small, start-up nonprofit organizations, you may only have a small amount of cash on-hand at the time of application.

Several categories on the statement of revenues and expenses and the balance sheet require that you attach an itemized list. The form indicates when this is required. Make sure you remember to attach it to your final application.

Form 1023 requires the completion of various schedules depending on the type of organization that is applying for tax exemption. Here is a rundown:

* Schedule A—Churches
* Schedule B—Schools, Colleges, and Universities
* Schedule C—Hospitals and Medical Research Organizations
* Schedule D—Section 509(a)(3) Supporting Organizations
* Schedule E—Organizations Not Filing Form 1023 Within 27 Months of Formation
* Schedule F—Homes for the Elderly or Handicapped and Low-Income Housing
* Schedule G—Successors to Other Organizations
* Schedule H—Organizations Providing Scholarships, Educational Loans, or Other Educational Grants

After the completion of Form 1023, your financials with itemized details (if required), and any required schedules, you are ready to package your application to send to the Internal Revenue Service.

Mailing Address

As of December 2011, the mailing address for your completed application package is:

Internal Revenue Service
P.O. Box 12192
Covington, KY 41012-0192

Filing Fee

The IRS increased the user fees for all Form 1023 applications post-marked after January 3, 2010. The current fees are:

* $400 for organizations whose gross receipts do not exceed $10,000 or less annually over a 4-year period.

* $850 for organizations whose gross receipts exceed $10,000 annually over a 4-year period.

To ensure that the filing fees remain as stated above, you can perform a search at the IRS's website or you can also call them at 1-877-829-5500.

Remember to also check to see if the Cyber Assistant is available, which will offer dramatically reduced filing fees.

Chapter 9

The Ins and Outs of 501(c)(3) Status

*"I am of the opinion that my life belongs to the community,
and as long as I live, it is my privilege to do for it whatever I can.
I want to be thoroughly used up when I die, for the harder I work,
the more I live. Life is no 'brief candle' to me. It is a sort of
splendid torch which I have got hold of for a moment, and
I want to make it burn as brightly as possible before
handing it on to future generations."*

~George Bernard Shaw

After the IRS reviews and processes your tax-exemption request application, you should expect to receive a written response indicating their determination. Of course, we anticipate a positive response and you will be notified that they have determined your organization to qualify for tax-exemption; or they may request additional information; or they will issue a proposed adverse determination, thus temporarily denying your request. You will have 30 days to appeal the adverse decision. At this point, you may choose to enlist a legal professional or continue to go it alone by reading and following the appeal procedures included in IRS Publication 557.

Once your request is approved and your organization is granted tax-exempt status, you will receive a Federal Determination Letter. First and foremost, you will want to celebrate! Your hard work has paid off and you are well on your way to serving your community.

Keep this important document in a safe place because it will be required for many purposes in the future. I highly recommend that you scan the document so the organization's staff will have access to an electronic copy when needed.

Having achieved this milestone, you will want to protect your status by filing all required reports in a timely manner. In 2011, 275,000 nonprofits lost their tax-exempt status for failure to file their annual reports. The announcement appears in the sidebar.

IR-2011-63, June 8, 2011

WASHINGTON — The Internal Revenue Service today announced that approximately 275,000 organizations under the law have automatically lost their tax-exempt status because they did not file legally required annual reports for three consecutive years. The IRS believes the vast majority of these organizations are defunct, but it also announced special steps to help any existing organizations to apply for reinstatement of their tax-exempt status.

Congress passed the Pension Protection Act (PPA) in 2006, requiring most tax-exempt organizations to file annual information returns or notice with the IRS. For small organizations, the law imposed a filing requirement for the first time in 2007. In addition, the law automatically revokes the tax-exempt status of any organization that does not file required returns or notices for three consecutive years.

For several years, the IRS has made an extensive effort to inform organizations of the changes in the law through multiple outreach and education avenues, including mailing more than 1 million notices to organizations that had not filed. In addition, last year the IRS published a list of at-risk groups and gave smaller organizations an additional five months to file required notices and come into compliance. About 50,000 organizations filed during this extension period. Overall, the IRS believes the vast majority of small tax-exempt organizations are now in compliance with the 2006 law.

"During the past several years, the IRS has gone the extra mile to help make tax-exempt groups aware of their legal filing requirement and allow them additional time to file," IRS Commissioner Doug Shulman said. "Still, we realize there may be some legitimate organizations, especially very small ones that were unaware of their new filing requirement. We are taking additional steps for these groups to maintain their tax-exempt status without jeopardizing their operations or harming their donors."

As part of this, the IRS issued guidance today on how organizations can apply for reinstatement of their tax-exempt status, including retroactive reinstatement. In addition, the IRS announced transition relief for certain small tax-exempt organizations—those with annual gross receipts of $50,000 or less for 2010— that were made subject to the new "postcard" filing under the PPA. The relief allows eligible small organizations to regain their tax-exempt status retroactive to the date of revocation and pay a reduced application fee of $100 rather than the typical $400 or $850 fee. Full details are available in Notice 2011-43, Notice 2011-44, and Revenue Procedure 2011-36, issued today.

If an organization appears on the list of organizations whose tax-exempt status has been automatically revoked, it is because IRS records indicate the organization had a filing requirement and did not file the required returns or notices for 2007, 2008, and 2009.

The list of organizations whose tax-exempt status has been revoked for failing to meet their filing requirement, available on the IRS website at www.IRS.gov, includes each organization's name, Employer Identification Number (EIN), and last known address. It is searchable by state. It also includes the effective date of the automatic revocation and the date it was posted to the list. The IRS will update the list monthly to include additional organizations that lose their tax-exempt status.

The vast majority of tax-exempt groups file their required returns and are unaffected by the revocation listing. In addition, the IRS believes the vast majority of the newly revoked groups are no longer in existence and need to be removed from the tax-exempt listing as the 2006 law requires.

This listing should have little, if any, impact on donors who previously made deductible contributions to auto-revoked organizations because donations made prior to the publication of an organization's name on the list remain tax-deductible. Going forward, however, organizations that are on the auto-revocation list that do not receive reinstatement are no longer eligible to receive tax-deductible contributions, and any income they receive may be taxable.

Publication on the list of organizations whose tax-exempt status has been revoked serves as notice to donors and others that they may no longer rely on a prior listing in IRS Publication 78, Cumulative List of Organizations, as an indication of an organization's tax-exempt status or its eligibility to receive tax-deductible contributions. An updated version of Publication 78 with current listings is available. Nor can donors rely on an IRS determination letter issued to the organization prior to the date of automatic revocation.

Existing organizations that seek to have their tax-exempt status reinstated must complete an application and pay a user fee regardless of whether they were originally required to file such an application. More information on the reinstatement process, including retroactive reinstatement, can be found on IRS.gov.

We can agree right now that you never want to find the name of your organization on the automatic revocation list. You have worked too hard to get to this point and you certainly don't want to have to do the additional work to have your organization reinstated. You and your board would have to do double-duty to repair the damage to your reputation in the community. It is extremely difficult to regain your donors' trust after this type of publicity.

Additional Filing Requirements

After receiving tax-exempt status designation from the federal government, you may need to apply for corporate income tax exemption from the state in which your organization will operate. Compared to the application process with the IRS, this should be much less time consuming.

You will also want to apply for exemption from local personal property taxes. This would apply to any real property that is owned or leased by the corporation (e.g., a leased copier/scanner machine).

Now you will want to verify the requirements for the state in which your organization will operate. Some states require nonprofits register with the attorney general as an organization that will be soliciting donations. This is typically in the consumer protection division of the attorney general's office. Contact information is provided in the last section of this book.

As you recall, tax-exempt organizations also qualify for reduced postage rates. You will need to fill out the required application, USPS Form 3624, *Application to Mail at Nonprofit Standard Mail Prices*, which is available online at: http://pe.usps.com/businessmail101/misc/nonprofitApplication.htm.

The website lists the supporting documents that you will need to provide when you submit your application to the U.S. Postal Service. Reduced postal rates will offer a great bottom-line cost savings if your organization will be mailing a large volume of printed communications (newsletters, event or program invitations, annual reports, etc.).

Record Keeping

To operate an effective and efficient business, you will want to ensure that your corporation's documents are secure and easily accessible when needed. With technology today, it should be easy to keep electronic copies of all of your important records. Copies of documents such as your board orientation manual, grant applications, bank applications, and audits will be needed in all types of situations.

You may choose to have a corporate manual to organize and store all of these documents. You can also start a binder to keep the minutes from all board and committee meetings. It is also a great policy to keep copies of all agendas and supporting documents, along with any written reports prepared by committee chairs. These documents could also be scanned and stored electronically.

Other Legal Landmines

Private Inurement

This is one of the most important tenants of nonprofit law. We previously incorporated the private inurement rule into our sample bylaws (and hopefully it appears in your bylaws):

Section 2 — No private inurement: No part of the net earnings of the corporation shall inure to the benefit of or be distributable to its members, trustees, officers, or other private persons, except that of the Corporation shall be authorized and empowered to pay reasonable compensation for services rendered and to make payments and distributions in furtherance of the purposes set forth in Section 1 hereof.

And of course, the official statement from the Internal Revenue Service states:

"No part of the net earnings of the organization shall inure to the benefit of, or be distributable to its members, trustees, officers, or other private persons, except that the organization shall be authorized and empowered to pay reasonable compensation for services rendered and to make payments and distributions in furtherance of the purposes set forth in the purpose clause hereof. No substantial part of the activities of the organization shall be the carrying on of propaganda, or otherwise attempting to influence legislation, and the organization shall not participate in, or intervene in (including the publishing or distribution of statements) any political campaign on behalf of any candidate for public office. Notwithstanding any other provision of this document, the organization shall not carry on any other activities not permitted to be carried on (a) by any organization exempt from federal income tax under section 501 (c) (3) of the Internal Revenue Code, corresponding section of any future federal tax code, or (b) by an organization, contributions to which are deductible under section 170 (c) (2) of the Internal Revenue Code, or corresponding section of any future federal tax code."

NOTE

For member organizations, the rule would be that whatever one member receives as a benefit must be received by all members.

Excess Benefit Transactions

As the leader of a nonprofit organization, you must ensure that all transactions are appropriate and at fair-market rates. Whether it be salaries paid to employees; rent paid to a landlord (perhaps even a director); or payment for services rendered, it will be your responsibility to ensure that the payments are at fair-market rates. The accounts payable vendor file or payroll records should include any supporting documentation that is appropriate, like a salary survey of other nonprofit organizations, a publication detailing local commercial rental rates, or competing bids for services.

Lobbying/Political Activities

Another way to put your organization's tax-exempt status in jeopardy is if it is determined that a substantial portion of your organization's activities are in an attempt to influence legislation or in propaganda. As you can imagine, it is important that you not cross this line.

The IRS allows a public charity (other than churches or its related affiliates) to voluntarily elect to replace the "substantial part of activities test" with a limit defined by the amount of dollars expended for the purpose of influencing legislation. Private foundations cannot make this election.

If an organization chooses to make the election, they will be required to complete IRS Form 5768 (Election/Revocation of Election By an Eligible Section 501(c)(3) Organization To Make Expenditures To Influence Legislation). The form must be signed and postmarked within the first tax year to which the election applies. The same form is used to revoke the election and must be signed and postmarked before the first day of the tax year to which it applies. Furthermore, the IRS stipulates that eligible section 501(c)(3) organizations making the election to be subject to the limits on lobbying expenditures use Part II-A of Schedule C (Form 990 or 990-EZ) to figure the limits.

The following information is from IRS Publication 557 (*Tax Exempt Status for Your Organization*, 10/2011):

Lobbying nontaxable amount. The lobbying nontaxable amount for any organization for any tax year is the lesser of $1,000,000 or:

* 20% of the exempt purpose expenditures if the exempt purpose expenditures are not over $500,000,

* $100,000 plus 15% of the excess of the exempt purpose expenditures over $500,000 if the exempt purpose expenditures are over $500,000 but not over $1,000,000,

* $175,000 plus 10% of the excess of the exempt purpose expenditures over $1,000,000 if the exempt purpose expenditures are over $1,000,000 but not over $1,500,000, or

* $225,000 plus 5% of the excess of the exempt purpose expenditures over $1,500,000 if the exempt purpose expenditures are over $1,500,000.

The term *exempt purpose expenditures* means the total of the amounts paid or incurred (including depreciation and amortization, but not capital expenditures) by an organization for the tax year to accomplish its exempt purposes. In addition, it includes:

* Administrative expenses paid or incurred for the organization's exempt purposes, and

* Amounts paid or incurred for the purpose of influencing legislation, whether or not the legislation promotes the organization's exempt purposes.

* Exempt purpose expenditures do not include amounts paid or incurred to or for:

    * A separate fundraising unit of the organization, or
    * One or more other organizations, if the amounts are paid or incurred primarily for fundraising.

Grass roots nontaxable amount. The grass roots nontaxable amount for any organization for any tax year is 25% of the lobbying nontaxable amount for the organization for that tax year.

Years for which election is effective. Once an organization elects to come under these provisions, the election will be in effect for all tax years that end after the date of the election and begin before the organization revokes this election.

Sarbanes-Oxley (SOX) Act Impact on Nonprofit Organizations

The Sarbanes-Oxley Act (enacted on July 30, 2002) was created in response to some high-profile corporate accounting scandals in the for-profit sector. Although the original intent was to boost the public's trust in the corporate sector, many nonprofits have strengthened their governance policies in light of SOX requirements. The following provisions should be adopted as part of your organization's policies and procedures.

There are several financial reporting responsibilities under the SOX Act that directly affect nonprofit organizations. They include:

* The audit committee responsibilities
* Auditor responsibilities
* Certified financial statements

These audit requirements will be discussed in detail in Chapter 12. In addition to these financial requirements, the following policies and procedures apply to employees of your organization, as well as board members.

Conflicts of Interest

According to the provisions of the Sarbanes-Oxley Act, your organization must have a written conflict of interest policy for your employees, volunteers, and members of your board of directors. Not only does this make good business sense, your auditors will ask for a copy of your written policy since it is a SOX requirement.

Some conflicts of interest should obviously prevent potential board members from serving on your board or an applicant from joining the staff of your nonprofit organization. Other conflicts may be of a nature that just precludes a director from voting on a particular contract or issue.

It is the best policy to document any potential or known conflicts of interest. You and your board should have a candid discussion regarding any reported conflicts.

A sample policy and disclosure form for your board of directors is provided. It can be easily amended to use for your staff and volunteer corps.

SAMPLE
CONFLICT OF INTEREST POLICY

It is in the best interest of _____, a nonprofit corporation, to be aware of and properly manage all conflicts of interest and appearances of a conflict of interest. This conflict of interest policy is designed to help directors, officers, employees, and volunteers of the organization identify situations that present potential conflicts of interest and to provide the organization with a procedure to appropriately manage conflicts in accordance with legal requirements and the goals of accountability and transparency in the organization's operations.

1. **CONFLICT OF INTEREST DEFINED.** In this policy, a person with a conflict of interest is referred to as an "interested person." For purposes of this policy, the following circumstances shall be deemed to create a Conflict of Interest:

   a. A director, officer, employee, or volunteer, including a board member (or family member of any of the foregoing) is a party to a contract, or involved in a transaction with **the organization** for goods or services.

   b. A director, officer, employee, or volunteer (or a family member of any of the foregoing) has a material financial interest in a transaction between **the organization** and an entity in which the director, officer, employee, or volunteer, or a family member of the foregoing, is a director, officer, agent, partner, associate, employee, trustee, personal representative, receiver, guardian, custodian, or other legal representative.

   c. A director, officer, employee, or volunteer (or a family member of the foregoing) is engaged in some capacity or has a material financial interest in a business or enterprise that competes with **the organization**.

(continued)

CONFLICT OF INTEREST POLICY*(continued)*

Other situations may create the appearance of a conflict, or present a duality of interests in connection with a person who has influence over the activities or finances of the nonprofit. All such circumstances should be disclosed to the board or staff, as appropriate, and a decision made as to what course of action the organization or individuals should take so that the best interests of the nonprofit are not compromised by the personal interests of stakeholders in the nonprofit.

Gifts, Gratuities, and Entertainment. Accepting gifts, entertainment, or other favors from individuals or entities can also result in a conflict or duality of interest when the party providing the gift/entertainment/favor does so under circumstances where it might be inferred that such action was intended to influence or possibly would influence the interested person in the performance of his or her duties. This does not preclude the acceptance of items of nominal or insignificant value or entertainment of nominal or insignificant value which are not related to any particular transaction or activity of **the organization**.

2. **DEFINITIONS.**
    a. A "Conflict of Interest" is any circumstance described in Part 1 of this policy.
    b. An "Interested Person" is any person serving as an officer, employee, or member of the board of directors of the organization or a major donor to the organization or anyone else who is in a position of control over the organization who has a personal interest that is in conflict with the interests of the organization.
    c. A "Family Member" is a spouse, parent, child, or spouse of a child, brother, sister, or spouse of a brother or sister, of an interested person.
    d. A "Material Financial Interest" in an entity is a financial interest of any kind, which, in view of all the circumstances, is substantial enough that it would, or reasonably could, affect an Interested Person's or Family Member's judgment with respect to transactions to which the entity is a party.

(continued)

CONFLICT OF INTEREST POLICY *(continued)*

e. A "Contract or Transaction" is any agreement or relationship involving the sale or purchase of goods or services, the providing or receipt of a loan or grant, the establishment of any other type of financial relationship, or the exercise of control over another organization. The making of a gift to the organization is not a Contract or Transaction.

f. "Nominal or Clearly Insignificant" is generally considered less than $50.

3. **PROCEDURES.**

a. Prior to board or committee action on a Contract or Transaction involving a Conflict of Interest, a director or committee member having a Conflict of Interest and who is in attendance at the meeting shall disclose all facts material to the Conflict of Interest. Such disclosure shall be reflected in the minutes of the meeting. If board members are aware that staff or other volunteers have a Conflict of Interest, relevant facts should be disclosed by the board member or by the interested person him/herself if invited to the board meeting as a guest for purposes of disclosure.

b. A director or committee member who plans not to attend a meeting at which he or she has reason to believe that the board or committee will act on a matter in which the person has a Conflict of Interest shall disclose to the chair of the meeting all facts material to the Conflict of Interest. The chair shall report the disclosure at the meeting and the disclosure shall be reflected in the minutes of the meeting.

c. A person who has a Conflict of Interest shall not participate in or be permitted to hear the board's or committee's discussion of the matter except to disclose material facts and to respond to questions. Such person shall not attempt to exert his or her personal influence with respect to the matter, either at or outside the meeting.

(continued)

CONFLICT OF INTEREST POLICY *(continued)*

d. A person who has a Conflict of Interest with respect to a Contract or Transaction that will be voted on at a meeting shall not be counted in determining the presence of a quorum for purposes of the vote.

e. The person having a Conflict of Interest may not vote on the Contract or Transaction and shall not be present in the meeting room when the vote is taken, unless the vote is by secret ballot. Such person's ineligibility to vote shall be reflected in the minutes of the meeting. For purposes of this paragraph, a member of the board of directors of **the organization** has a Conflict of Interest when he or she stands for election as an officer or for re-election as a member of the board of directors.

f. Interested Persons who are not members of the board of directors of **the organization**, or who have a Conflict of Interest with respect to a Contract or Transaction that is not the subject of board or committee action, shall disclose to their supervisor, or the chair, or the chair's designee, any Conflict of Interest that such Interested Person has with respect to a Contract or Transaction. Such disclosure shall be made as soon as the Conflict of Interest is known to the Interested Person. The Interested Person shall refrain from any action that may affect **the organization's** participation in such Contract or Transaction. In the event it is not entirely clear that a Conflict of Interest exists, the individual with the potential conflict shall disclose the circumstances to his or her supervisor or the chair or the chair's designee, who shall determine whether full board discussion is warranted or whether there exists a Conflict of Interest that is subject to this policy.

3. **CONFIDENTIALITY.** Each director, officer, employee, and volunteer shall exercise care not to disclose confidential information acquired in connection with disclosures of conflicts of interest or potential conflicts, which might be adverse to the interests of the organization.

(continued)

CONFLICT OF INTEREST POLICY *(continued)*

Furthermore, directors, officers, employees, and volunteers shall not disclose or use information relating to the business of the organization for their personal profit or advantage or the personal profit or advantage of their Family Member(s).

3. **REVIEW OF POLICY.**

    a. Each director, officer, employee, and volunteer shall be provided with and asked to review a copy of this policy and to acknowledge in writing that he or she has done so.

    b. Annually each director, officer, employee, and volunteer shall complete a disclosure form identifying any relationships, positions, or circumstances in which s/he is involved that he or she believes could contribute to a Conflict of Interest. Such relationships, positions, or circumstances might include service as a director of or consultant to another nonprofit organization, or ownership of a business that might provide goods or services to **the organization**. Any such information regarding the business interests of a director, officer, employee, or volunteer, or a Family Member thereof, shall be treated as confidential and shall generally be made available only to the chair, the executive director, and any committee appointed to address Conflicts of Interest, except to the extent additional disclosure is necessary in connection with the implementation of this policy.

    c. This policy shall be reviewed annually by each member of the board of directors. Any changes to the policy shall be communicated to all staff and volunteers.

Conflict of Interest Disclosure

No member of **the organization's** board of directors (or family member of a director) shall derive any personal profit or gain, directly or indirectly, by reason of his or her participation in the organization. Each individual shall disclose to the organization any personal interest which he/she (or family member of director) may have in any matter pending before the organization and shall refrain from participation in any decision on such matter.

Other situations may create the appearance of a conflict, or present a duality of interests in connection with a person who has influence over the activities or finances of **the organization**. All such circumstances should be disclosed to the board and a decision made as to what course of action should be taken so that the best interests of **the organization** are not compromised by the personal interests of a member of the board of directors.

Any member of the organization's board of directors shall refrain from obtaining any list of the organization's clients or donors for personal or private solicitation purposes at any time during the term of their affiliation, and shall also refrain from discussing or sharing donor financial or corporate sponsorship information.

In addition to my service for **the organization**, at this time I am a board member or an employee of the following organizations:

1.

2.

This is to certify that I, except with regard to carrying out my duties as an officer, director, or staff member of **the organization** or as described below, am not now nor at any time during the past year have been:

1) A participant, directly or indirectly, in any arrangement, agreement, investment, or other activity with any vendor, supplier, or other party; doing business with **the organization** which has resulted or could result in personal benefit to me.

(continued)

Conflict of Interest Disclosure *(continued)*

2) A recipient, directly or indirectly, of any salary payments or loans or gifts of any kind or any free service or discounts or other fees from or on behalf of any person or organization engaged in any transaction with **the organization**.

Any exceptions to 1 or 2 above are stated below with a full description of the transactions and of the interest, whether direct or indirect, which I have (or have had during the past year) in the persons or organizations having transactions with **the organization**. Disclosure of exceptions to 1 and 2:

_____

_____

Signature:_____

Date_____

Printed Name:_____

Whistleblower Policy

In addition to a conflicts of interest policy, SOX also requires that corporations have a written whistleblower protection policy that discourages the criminal act of retaliation in response to a whistleblower's complaint. The executive staff and board of directors must not tolerate misconduct by anyone associated with your organization and must diligently follow up on any complaints. The organization should complete and document a thorough investigation, whether any corrective action is required or not.

Feel free to use the sample policy below or edit as you deem necessary. You and your board must select and share the contact information for the compliance officer; often the chair of the finance/audit committee serves in this capacity.

SAMPLE WHISTLEBLOWER POLICY

GENERAL

_____ (Organization) Code of Ethics and Conduct ("Code") requires directors, officers, and employees to observe high standards of business and personal ethics in the conduct of their duties and responsibilities. As employees and representatives of the organization, we must practice honesty and integrity in fulfilling our responsibilities and comply with all applicable laws and regulations.

REPORTING RESPONSIBILITY

It is the responsibility of all directors, officers, and employees to comply with the Code and to report violations or suspected violations in accordance with this Whistleblower Policy.

NO RETALIATION

No director, officer, or employee who in good faith reports a violation of the Code shall suffer harassment, retaliation, or adverse employment consequence. An employee who retaliates against someone who has reported a violation in good faith is subject to discipline up to and including termination of employment. This Whistleblower Policy is intended to encourage and enable employees and others to raise serious concerns within the organization prior to seeking resolution outside the organization.

REPORT VIOLATIONS

The Code addresses the organization's open door policy and suggests that employees share their questions, concerns, suggestions, or complaints with someone who can address them properly. In most cases, an employee's supervisor is in the best position to address an area of concern. However, if you are not comfortable speaking with your supervisor or you are not satisfied with your supervisor's response, you are encouraged to speak with someone in the Human Resources Department or anyone in management whom you are comfortable in approaching. Supervisors and managers are required to report suspected violations of the Code of Conduct to the organization's Compliance Officer, who has specific and exclusive responsibility to investigate all reported violations. For suspected fraud, or when

(continued)

SAMPLE WHISTLEBLOWER POLICY *(continued)*

you are not satisfied or uncomfortable with following the organization's open door policy, individuals should contact the organization's Compliance Officer directly.

COMPLIANCE OFFICER

The organization's Compliance Officer is responsible for investigating and resolving all reported complaints and allegations concerning violations of the Code and, at his/her discretion, shall advise the organization's chief executive, chairperson of the board of directors, and the executive committee. The Compliance Officer has direct access to the executive committee of the board of directors and is required to report to the executive committee at least annually on compliance activity. The organization's Compliance Officer is the chair of the finance/audit committee.

ACCOUNTING AND AUDITING MATTERS

The Finance Committee of the board of directors shall address all reported concerns or complaints regarding corporate accounting practices, internal controls, or auditing. The Compliance Officer shall immediately notify the Finance Committee of any such complaint and work with the Committee until the matter is resolved.

ACTING IN GOOD FAITH

Anyone filing a complaint concerning a violation or suspected violation of the Code must be acting in good faith and have reasonable grounds for believing the information disclosed indicates a violation of the Code. Any allegations that prove not to be substantiated and which prove to have been made maliciously or knowingly to be false will be viewed as a serious disciplinary offense.

CONFIDENTIALITY

Violations or suspected violations may be submitted on a confidential basis by the complainant or may be submitted anonymously. Reports of violations or suspected violations will be kept confidential to the extent possible, consistent with the need to conduct an adequate investigation.

(continued)

SAMPLE WHISTLEBLOWER POLICY *(continued)*

HANDLING OF REPORTED VIOLATIONS
The Compliance Officer will notify the sender and acknowledge receipt of the reported violation or suspected violation within five business days. All reports will be promptly investigated and appropriate corrective action will be taken if warranted by the investigation.

_____   _____
Compliance Officer   Human Resources Manager

CONTACT INFORMATION
Human Resources Manager:
Compliance Officer:

Document Destruction

The Sarbanes-Oxley Act also outlines the recommended schedule for document retention and destruction. The types of documents covered by SOX include financial records, contracts, real estate and other legal transactions, personnel files, client records, and development/fundraising documents. These important business records should be maintained according to the written guidelines established by the corporation. You should plan to have a secure (locked, with limited access) storage area large enough to house your archived documents.

Sample
Record Retention and Document Destruction Policy

The organization shall retain records for the period of their immediate or current use, unless longer retention is necessary for historical reference or to comply with contractual or legal requirements. Records and documents outlined in this policy include paper, electronic files (including e-mail), and voicemail records regardless of where the document is stored, including network servers, desktop or laptop computers and handheld computers, and other wireless devices with text messaging capabilities.

In accordance with 18 U.S.C. Section 1519 and the Sarbanes-Oxley Act, the organization shall not knowingly destroy a document with the intent to obstruct or influence an "investigation or proper administration of any matter within the jurisdiction of any department agency of the United States, or in relation to or contemplation of such matter or case." If an official investigation is underway or even suspected, document purging must stop in order to avoid criminal obstruction.

In order to eliminate accidental or innocent destruction, the organization has the following document retention policy:

Type of Document	Retention Period
Accounts receivable and payable ledgers and schedules	7 years
Annual audited financial statements, audit reports, general ledgers, internal audit reports	Permanently
Articles of incorporation, charter, bylaws, minutes, and other incorporation records	Permanently
Bank reconciliations	3 years minimum

(continued)

Record Retention and Document Destruction Policy
(continued)

Type of Document	Retention Period
Bank statements, deposit records, EFT documents, cancelled checks	3 years minimum
Chart of accounts	Permanently
Contracts, mortgages, notes, and leases (still in effect)	Permanently
Contracts, mortgages, notes, and leases (expired)	7 years
Correspondence (general)	3 years
Correspondence (legal and important matters)	Permanently
Depreciation schedules	Permanently
Employment applications	3 years from making the record or taking personnel action
Expense reports	7 years
Garnishments	7 years
Insurance policies, records, accident reports, and claims (expired)	Permanently
Inventory records	7 years
Invoices (to customers, from vendors)	7 years
Loan documents and notes	Permanently
Personnel files (employee demographic information and compensation records)	7 years

(continued)

Record Retention and Document Destruction Policy
(continued)

Type of Document	Retention Period
Personnel files (I-9s)	7 years after date of hire or 1 year after termination
Personnel files (payroll records and summaries, including records related to employee leave)	7 years
Personnel files (terminated employees)	7 years after termination
Retirement and pension records including summary plan descriptions (ERISA)	Permanently
Tax returns (990s) and worksheets	Permanently
Timesheets	7 years
Trademark registration and copyrights	Permanently
Workers' compensation documentation	10 years after 1st closure

This policy should be included in your accounting policies and procedures, as well as the employee manual given to all employees to ensure that the organization's important business documents are protected from inadvertent destruction.

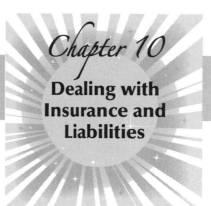

Chapter 10

Dealing with Insurance and Liabilities

"The happiest people I have known have been those who gave themselves no concern about their own souls, but did their uttermost to mitigate the miseries of others."

~Elizabeth Cady Stanton

The requirements for your nonprofit organization can seem overwhelming. It is critical that you surround yourself with trusted advisors and the most qualified staff members, volunteers, and board members you can find. These talented and dedicated people will help lighten your load and protect your organization.

When considering the different types of insurance for your nonprofit, you will find that the coverage falls into one of these categories:

* Statutory
* Contractual
* Optional

Statutory

Statutory insurance is exactly what you would deduce. These are the types of insurance that your state requires, like worker's compensation or unemployment benefits. If your organization's employees or volunteers will be driving agency-owned vehicles, auto insurance is also a must.

To find out what corporate insurance is required in your state, you may contact the secretary of state's office (contact information is available in the appendix of this book) or by contacting a trusted insurance professional in your community. I would certainly recommend asking your board members and community partners for referrals. It is in your best interest to find an agent that has experience working with nonprofit organizations. Another option is to join a professional, business, or membership organization in your community. Often, your local chamber of commerce or similar organizations provide opportunities for lower-rate insurance for its members.

Contractual

Depending on the types of funding and funding sources your agency receives, you may be contractually required to carry certain types of insurance. This may include general liability insurance, professional liability, or employee crime/theft. The grant contract will state the contractual insurance requirements for your organization.

Most times, the grantor will ask for a certificate of insurance naming their agency as an additional insured. Your insurance agent will be able to provide these certificates. Keep a copy of the certificate in your files.

Directors' and Officers'

The most common type of optional insurance is directors' and officers' liability insurance (D & O). Some potential board members will ask about the existence of this type of insurance before considering joining your board. As a new organization, it may be difficult to afford this type of insurance.

Directors' and officers' liability insurance basically defends the board members from claims of failing to fulfill their responsibilities or poor management.

Umbrella Insurance

Umbrella liability insurance adds additional coverage levels beyond the primary policy limits. This is typically very reasonably priced and offers your organization more protection.

I recommend that you ask other nonprofit organizations in your community for a referral to an insurance agent that has experience working with nonprofits. An insurance agent would make a good addition to your board of directors.

Liabilities

Although your intent is to create a nonprofit organization, you will still have multiple types of liabilities. The most common will be employment-related taxes.

Payroll Taxes

Besides occupancy costs, most nonprofits' largest expense line item is salaries and wages for their employees. The associated liabilities for paying your staff will be payroll taxes.

Federal taxes will be withheld from your employees' earnings, and the organization will also pay social security and Medicare taxes, as well as unemployment taxes required by the state in which your organization will operate.

Another benefit to organizations exempt from income tax under section 501(c)(3) of the Internal Revenue Code is that they are also exempt from federal unemployment tax or FUTA. According to the IRS, this exemption cannot be waived.

FUTA is part of a combined federal and state program that pays unemployment compensation to those who lose their jobs. The federal unemployment program was created in an effort to encourage states to provide payment to employees that find themselves unemployed. FUTA tax is an organizational liability, thus employees do not pay any portion of this tax and it cannot be withheld from their pay.

Sales Tax

If your organization operates a social enterprise, like a gift shop, you will be responsible for collecting and paying sales tax.

Chapter 11

Hiring: Finding the Right Talent for the Job

---

*"The future belongs to those who believe
in the beauty of their dreams."*

~Eleanor Roosevelt

In addition to the time and effort you've invested in this project so far, hopefully you have also done a personal skills assessment. It is important that you find talented people to join your organization (as employees or volunteers) that can provide expertise in the areas that are not your strong suit.

Rarely do nonprofit organizations have the budget to hire all of the employees that are required to adequately handle all of the needed functions. During your environmental scanning process, you should have learned the basic organizational structure of similar agencies. You will need to have employees to fulfill the following tasks: administration, accounting, development, and service or program delivery. As your organization grows, you will likely add staff in maintenance, information technology, and operations.

Each position should have a written job description that should be reviewed and updated annually. You could research local and national job boards to help in drafting job descriptions. When employees are hired, you should have the new hire sign a copy of their job description to keep in their permanent employee file.

Background Checks

Another best practice is to conduct a background screening before an employee or volunteer begins working for your organization. There are online services, as well as agencies that will conduct personal interviews and background checks. Your agency's services and clients will dictate the type of screenings required. Pre-employment screenings may include drug testing, verification of certifications and education, verification of previous employment, financial credit verification, and driving/criminal history. You will want to have a policy in place that states in what cases an applicant would be ineligible for employment.

Salaries

You will want to ensure that you are paying appropriate wages for all of your employees. There are organizations that conduct and publish nonprofit salary surveys. You may have access to a current survey through one of your partner organizations or a board member. If you are unable to borrow a survey, it would be a good idea for your organization to purchase a copy of the survey.

The surveys will show the minimum salary, the average, and the highest salary for each job. Of course, you will also need to consider each applicant's qualifications when determining the employment offer.

In the beginning, you will likely be hiring at the lower end of the salary range. Unfortunately, you may find that once your employees gain a certain level of experience, they will qualify for higher paying positions in "competing" organizations.

I recommend that you purchase a salary survey every other year to ensure that you are paying market rates for your employees. They are the organization's most valuable asset and it is very costly to have continual turnover.

The auditors may inquire how the board reviews the chief executive's salary. A current salary survey is confirmation that the board remains committed to providing excellent oversight and ensures that the corporation is paying fair market rates. You can expect to pay a fee to purchase current nonprofit salary surveys, but the information will be well worth the expense. In my community, the most extensive surveys provide comparisons between two metropolitan cities and are based on the size of the surveyed organization's budget.

This makes it easy to compare "apples to apples" when reviewing your staff's salaries. These surveys are conducted on a routine basis (perhaps every two years) by nonprofit associations. A quick Google search should provide a couple of options for you to review.

Benefits

Even though you may not be able to afford to pay at the top of the salary range, you may be able to offer attractive benefits for your employees. While my daughter was in elementary and junior high school, I was able to divide my time between working in the office and telecommuting from home. As a working mother, this benefit was priceless. I was able to save the cost of daycare and spend more time with my daughter—it is still hard for me to place a value on this benefit.

Besides part-time employment and telecommuting, you may consider job-sharing opportunities and generous leave policies. If your operations allow, perhaps you could permit employees to bring their children to work with them.

This is an area in which using your creativity and flexibility could help your agency attract the most talented workforce.

Schedules

Nonprofit organizations, just like for-profit corporations, vary in the requirements for employee coverage. Your services and clients will determine the days and hours your organization will be open and serving the community. Some nonprofits have Monday through Friday operations, while others will operate 24 hours a day/365 days per year.

You will want to take this into account when determining the number of employees and volunteers you will need to employ to properly fulfill your mission.

Contract Employees and Volunteers

In the early stages of your nonprofit, you may find the option of contract employees very attractive. This arrangement will allow flexibility in determining the work hours and will not require you to pay employment-related taxes or provide benefits. Make sure to check with your state's employment commission to ensure that you follow all required guidelines for contract labor. At year-end, you will report the amount of money paid to your contractors by providing them with IRS Form 1099.

The most cost-effective option is to engage volunteers to fulfill some of the responsibilities within your organization. Your volunteer corps will require a great deal of management and training, so you and your staff will need to allocate enough time to make this arrangement successful. You may find that a large percentage of your volunteers are between paid jobs—meaning they may find a paid position and you will need to replace them as your volunteer. If the timing is right, you may be able to transition a hardworking and talented volunteer into a paid position within your organization!

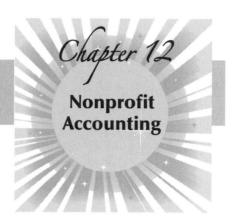

Chapter 12

Nonprofit Accounting

"There is a tremendous strength that is growing in the world through...sharing together, praying together, suffering together, and working together."

~Mother Teresa

Although you're passionate about providing needed services in your community, you and your team will have to properly administer the not-so-glamorous business aspects of your new organization. If accounting is not your forte, heed my advice and hire the most qualified candidate you can afford to manage the financial functions. It will be a very costly mistake to allow a lapse in the organization's accounting responsibilities to occur.

Depending on your organization's funding sources, the accounting records for your organization will need to comply with the following:

* GAAP (Generally Accepted Accounting Principles)
* OMB Circular A-110: Uniform Administrative Requirements for Grants and Agreements with Institutions of Higher Education, Hospitals, and Other Non-Profit Organizations
* OMB Circular A-122: Cost Principles for Non-Profit Organizations
* OMB Circular A-133: Audits of States, Local Governments, and Non-Profit Organizations

* GASB 34 (Governmental Accounting Standards Board): Basic Financial Statements and Management's Discussion and Analysis for State and Local Governments

It is important to have a detailed accounting policies and procedures manual. I will hit some of the high points in this chapter, but you may want to ask a couple of your partner agencies for a copy of their manual. Established non-profits are well aware of the financial constraints of new agencies and are often willing to share their internal business documents. Make sure to return the favor in the future.

Responsibilities

Your policies and procedures should clearly define the roles and responsibilities of all persons involved in the accounting process. Most likely, it will include the board of directors, the chief executive, the administrative staff, and the accounting manager and/or staff.

General Policies

This section will provide for the basic business function of your organization. You should draft policies that provide for accurate business records, for example:

* Job descriptions for each position
* Separation of duties (primarily relating to cash receipts, payroll, bank reconciliations, accounts payable, or other accounting functions)
* Timesheets are computer generated or completed in ink and signed by a supervisor

Budgets

When you prepared your Form 1023 application, you drafted pro forma (forecast) budgets for your organization for the first three years. Keep in mind that a budget is your best estimate of the income and expenses you anticipate within the budget period. On a monthly basis, you or your accounting manager should prepare financials comparing the actual results to the projected budget for that month or period.

Incorporate your programs and plans into your annual budget. Since you will not have a history on which to base your assumptions, you may want to rely on your trusted advisors to share information from similar events. This is another area where I like to be conservative by "under promising," which will allow you to "over deliver" when you exceed the original revenue goals.

Board Approval

Once you and your staff feel confident about the budget you've developed, it should be presented to the finance committee for their input. After incorporating their suggestions and making any recommended adjustments, the treasurer will present to the full board at their next meeting. Ensure that the board formally accepts the budget and that the approval appears in the minutes of the meeting.

Your projections may change from month to month, but your approved budget should remain stagnant. It will be used as a planning tool and to measure the success of you and your employees' work toward the fulfillment of your organization's mission.

Variances, Remedies, and Contingencies

On a monthly basis, the accounting manager and/or chief executive should prepare a narrative report to discuss any budget variances, propose remedies, and offer a contingency plan if the deficiency cannot be immediately resolved. Never offer a remedy you do not want to execute—once you've put it on the table, you may be forced to follow through with your proffer.

More than once, I have witnessed an overwhelmed chief executive threaten to quit his job over one challenge or another. Imagine the shock when the board of directors soon thereafter asked for a resignation letter.

Choosing Accounting Software

In the very beginning, you may find Excel works fine during the planning phase of your new nonprofit. But once you're off and running, you will want to purchase accounting software. Many start-up organizations use over-the-counter software packages, like Peachtree, Quicken, or QuickBooks. Personally, I am a fan of QuickBooks for Nonprofits, which is user-friendly and will help you in developing an initial basic chart of accounts. QuickBooks also offers a Point-of-Sale (POS) software program that could be used in retail social enterprises.

At some point, your organization will likely want to invest in development software to aid in keeping up with your donors' information. Some of the most commonly used software companies (Blackbaud, Sage) have companion financial packages. This would allow your development and accounting information to flow seamlessly between the departments.

Accounting Policies and Procedures

From the beginning, your organization's leadership team will need to develop a written set of policies and procedures for your accounting functions. I encourage you to ask other organizations or even your accounting firm for a sample copy of nonprofit internal controls. Here are the highlights:

Internal Controls

Internal controls will be the set of policies and procedures that ensure the organization's assets are secure and properly protected. When and if you select an accounting firm to work with your organization, they will be able to provide guidance and may even have some examples of other nonprofit organization's internal control procedures. The following sections will provide a broad overview as a starting point for you and your organization.

Accounts Receivable/Cash Receipts

The policy should address what forms of receipts your organization will receive and in what form (cash, credit cards, checks, etc.). Be clear about the procedure for opening and distributing incoming mail. Your procedure should state which position is charged with the act of opening mail, which position is responsible for logging the receipts, and who will be processing the receipts for deposit.

After the receipts are accepted by the accounting department, the procedure should include endorsing checks and keeping items for deposit secure (locked drawer, safe, etc.) until taken to the bank for deposit.

Copies of all items for deposit, along with any letters or check stubs, should be made and delivered to the development department for entry into their database and the mailing of a donor thank-you letter/tax receipt.

To properly safeguard your organization's receipts, deposits should be made frequently. The procedure should indicate who is responsible for taking deposits to the bank and, after the receipt is attached to the accounting department's copy, who will enter the deposit into the accounting system.

An easy way to file your financial records is to store all the records in a large manila envelope by month. The accounting department would file all copies of deposits with receipts attached, the bank statement with the reconciliation report, and any electronic deposits or debits.

The chief executive should review the reconciled bank statements and initial along with the accounting person responsible for this process.

Record of Receipts

I find it helpful if the person charged with opening the mail sends an email to the accounting and development staff with a list of the day's receipts. This provides a lasting record, a receipt book of sorts.

Petty Cash

Petty cash allows employees to make small purchases or reimbursements without going through the process of accounts payable. The petty cash should be of a nominal amount and stored in a secure location. Petty cash should be balanced (replenished) on a monthly basis. The accounting manager or chief executive should perform periodic unannounced audits of the petty cash.

Accounts Payable

Disbursement policies and procedures ensure that all payables are supported by proper documentation and authorization.

Your accounting policies should state clearly who is allowed to authorize payables or expenditures and at what amount.

Payroll

Payroll is one of the areas that your organization could be vulnerable to improper activities by an employee; therefore you can expect your auditors to review a large sample of transactions.

Your policies should state:

* Pay frequency for employees
* Procedures for completing timesheets (specifying cost center or grant, if required)
* Guidelines for authorizing time sheets
* Salary change procedures (new hires, pay increases/decreases, changes in deductions)

Grant Proposals and Reports

Grant proposals and reports require the collaboration of several departments, except in the beginning when you may have just one or two employees! Writing the proposal may include input from the following departments:

* Chief executive
* Development department
* Program department
* Accounting department
* Marketing department

The policy should indicate that all contract and grant documents will be reviewed and approved by the accounting manager (and any other appropriate staff members) prior to being signed by the chief executive.

Original copies of signed grants and contracts are filed by the accounting department with copies to the development department and program staff. If you have the technological ability to scan a copy of the grant contract, it would be handy to have it available electronically for staff.

The preparation of reports, payment requests, and/or invoices will typically involve several departments. The accounting department will prepare the financials; the executive and development department will likely write the narrative overview; and the program staff will deliver the program outcomes/deliverables.

The majority of grantors will supply grant recipients with electronic or preprinted forms for completion and submission. Make sure you keep all due dates on your calendar. Missing a report deadline could jeopardize your organization's future funding.

Fund Accounting for Grants

Whatever accounting system you chose, it will be necessary to have a system to keep grant funds separated. In QuickBooks, you can accomplish this by using one chart of accounts and also assigning each funding source a "class." This allows you to track the revenue and expenses from each funding source. It is a breeze to run P & L reports by class, which will be extremely helpful in developing any required grant reports.

Financials

As a nonprofit organization, it will be incumbent upon you and your board of directors to provide transparent and accurate financial information to interested parties in the community. Your finance committee should work closely with the chief executive and accounting staff to develop the financial reports that will be provided in the packet at each board meeting. The following sections will provide an overview of the other financials.

Profit and Loss

Your new organization will be providing basic financial statements to the board of directors, potential funders, banks, and other lending institutions. You will find that different agencies have different names for the P & L. Some will request an Income Statement or even a Statement of Operations. This report will show your organization's revenue and expenses.

Balance Sheet

In addition to the P & L, your organization will also be required to provide a Balance Sheet that details the assets and liabilities. Sometimes this report is referred to as a Statement of Financial Condition since it reflects the net of the organization's assets and liabilities.

OMB Circulars

Directives are issued by the Office of Management and Budget (OMB) to federal agencies, and in some cases, the recipients of federal awards. Two of the most common applicable directives for nonprofit organizations are OMB A-110 and A-133.

A-110: OMB Circular A-110 addresses the uniform administrative requirements for grants and agreements with institutions of higher education, hospitals, and other nonprofit organizations. The intent of this circular is to clearly define the requirements for recipients of federal grants.

A-122: OMB Circular A-122 establishes principles for determining costs of grants, contracts, and other agreements between nonprofit organizations and the federal government. The principles state that the federal government pays its fair share of costs unless otherwise restricted or prohibited by law.

A-133: OMB Circular A-133 or the Single Audit Act requires recipients (specifically states, local governments, and nonprofit organizations) that expend more than $500,000 in federal awards to elect a Single Audit or Program-Specific Audit.

A single audit will be conducted in conjunction with your regularly scheduled external audit. If you receive multiple federal awards (good for you!), the auditors will randomly select one of the grants to audit following the guidelines of OMB A-133. As you can imagine, your auditor's fee will reflect the additional time required to complete the in-depth examination.

Audit (It's Just a Five-Letter Word)

As your organization grows, it may become necessary to conduct an annual external audit to satisfy many of your private funders, as well as municipal and federal funders. If your organization expends more than $500,000 in federal funds, an A-133 or single audit will be required.

The purpose of the external audit is to ensure that your organization is properly safeguarding its assets and following Generally Accepted Accounting Principles in all financial reporting activities. While the audit can be a stressful experience, it need not be.

Policy and Procedure

The finance committee should determine the type of audit requirement based on the organization's funding and the frequency of the external examination. The finance committee may operate as the organization's audit committee.

From time to time, the finance/audit committee and organizational leadership should accept referrals from the full board as to accounting firms to approach for requests for proposal for the organization's external audit. I suggest that you interview three candidate firms. Upon completion of the interviews and receipt of the written proposals, the finance/audit committee will make their recommendation to the board based on the firm's experience, scope, and price quoted. Once the organization's leadership and board of directors agree on the firm, an engagement letter will be signed. Your written agreement with the firm should include a statement that the firm is to request approval prior to beginning any work that would exceed the original cost quoted. Make sure you keep this document with your important papers.

Audit Preparation

The selected audit firm will send the organization's designated accounting staff representative a list of documents required prior to the onsite commencement and documents needed once the auditors arrive at your offices. They will review bank statements, payables, receivables, pledges, grant documents, and board documents, to name a few.

When preparing for an audit, I usually begin by reconciling all of the balance sheet accounts. Your bank accounts should have been reconciled monthly, but you will also want to verify that your liability accounts, like your payroll liabilities and employee vacation accruals are reconciled, as well.

Another great preparation tactic is to run a general ledger for the year and review each transaction to ensure the expenses are charged to the correct general ledger account. If you choose to use the class system, you can run a profit and loss statement by class and reconcile to each grant.

I find it helpful to organize all of the documents that the auditors have requested in a box. That way, you will make a good first impression and the auditors can get right to work. It is best to have a private office or conference room for the auditors to use while onsite.

At some point near the end of the onsite portion of the audit, the senior partner will meet with the leadership team to give their initial impressions and discuss any pending requests and/or concerns. After the written audit results are prepared in draft form, they will be reviewed by the accounting team and the finance/audit committee. Upon their initial acceptance, the draft copy of the audit will be presented to the board of directors. Make sure the motion to accept the audit is entered into the minutes of the meeting.

Other Audits

Depending on the different types of funding your organization will receive, you may be subject to monitoring visits from the funding agencies. If you receive federal funds, you will likely be monitored on an annual basis.

Just like with the external audit, you will receive written notification of the date of the audit and the documents to be reviewed. If your organization provides services for clients, the monitoring visit will include a review of accounting documents, as well as direct service–related files. You should also expect a review of your employee files to ensure that the organization is following all federal hiring guidelines, conducting proper background verifications, and keeping accurate time sheets for billing.

Sarbanes-Oxley Act

There are multiple SOX guidelines that affect nonprofit organizations. As discussed in Chapter 9, your organization will need to have written policies for conflicts of interest, whistleblowers, and document destruction. You should expect your auditors to ask for copies of these documents.

In addition, SOX stipulates that you change audit partners or firms every five years. Many organizations choose to change firms, but you may find it more efficient to change audit partners instead. The purpose of this rule is to ensure that your audit firm does not become too comfortable or lax about your organization's procedures, which makes good business sense.

The Sarbanes-Oxley Act also recommends that the auditors discuss the organization's critical accounting policies and procedures with the finance/audit committee. It is likely that the content of the staff interviews will be disclosed to the committee.

Certified financial statements are another SOX requirement that applies to nonprofit organizations. This guideline is fulfilled by having the chief executive and the accounting manager or chief financial officer attest that the financial statements are a fair representation of the organization's financial position. The board, as the governing body, has the ultimate fiduciary responsibility for the integrity of the financial statements.

IRS Form 990

Oftentimes, the same accounting firm that conducts the audit will also prepare the organizations' IRS Form 990. A short time after the ratification of the audit report, the firm's tax department will complete the Form 990. The board should be given ample time to review the form and vote to accept the organization's Form 990.

As you recall, your Form 990 will be a public document and appear on the Internet. It is in your organization's best interest for the board of directors to be familiar with the contents of the tax report. Websites, like GuideStar, publish nonprofits' tax documents for donors or any interested party. This transparency is important and should instill the public's trust in the integrity of your organization.

Bottom Line

With the proper homework, preparation, and selection of an audit firm, your audit should be smooth sailing. You and your audit team should feel a great sense of accomplishment upon the completion of a successful audit process.

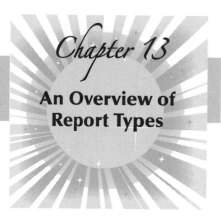

Chapter 13

An Overview of Report Types

> *"Only when we give joyfully, without hesitation or thought of gain, can we truly know what love means."*
>
> ~Leo Buscaglia

Managing a successful nonprofit will require numerous types of communication reports because of your different constituents. Your organization's stakeholders will include the public-at-large, your clients, your board of directors and other volunteers, your donors (current and potential), and your staff. Each audience will have questions and needs that are specific to their group.

As the nonprofit's leader, you will want to control the comprehensive message. All of your reports should share the same aspects of the overarching communication plan. For example, if you are building up to a milestone anniversary, your reports should highlight the achievements over the life of the agency. What are the biggest achievements—a million visitors, a thousand clients served—whatever important successes you choose to highlight should be reiterated in all of your organization's communications.

Accounting Reports

A variety of accounting reports will be prepared. The following will require accounting reports:

* Board of directors meetings
  * Budget
  * Budget to actual
  * Benchmarks

* Reports for leadership
  * Cash position
  * Outstanding payables and liabilities

* Grants
  * Proposals
  * Interim reports
  * Final reports

* Annual report published by the organization

Development Reports

The leadership and development teams are normally responsible for your agency's grant reports. The accounting department will prepare the financials, but the report will also require a great deal of narration to share the organization's successes and attainment of the strategic goals. I strongly advise you start by reviewing the initial grant request before completing an interim or final grant report to ensure you respond to the original goals identified.

Programmatic Reports

Programmatic reports will include the specific outcomes of any organizational programs. As we will discuss in the next section, there are different types of programs and therefore the expected outcomes will vary. These reports will have narrative portions, as well as statistical analysis of the participants' responses and overall attendance. These reports will be prepared for presentation to the board of directors, the funding agency and/or sponsors, and could also be used in the organization's annual report.

Management Reports

As you may have deduced by now, a great deal of your time will be spent on administrative duties like reporting. It can get frustrating and overwhelming at times because you will have so many competing priorities. The following sections provide an overview of some of the routine types of management reports you will be expected to provide.

Board Meetings

The leadership team will be expected to deliver professional and relevant reports during each board meeting. These reports should discuss benchmarks, financial, and programmatic outcomes and the status of the progress toward the attainment of any strategic goals.

In addition to the updates at board meetings, you will want to provide periodic updates for your board members. This may be in the form of an e-mail to the board—perhaps every other week—providing the board of directors with an interim update. This memo can be brief and focus on the latest success, maybe a positive grant proposal response or a standing-room-only program. A mention in the media (hopefully in a positive light) could be forwarded by sharing the link to the article or video. You will also want to get in front of any negative information, so address these items in your updates, also. This will help prepare your directors to answer questions they may encounter in the community.

Staff Meetings

Your staff will represent your organization in the community, so you'll want to ensure that they have the latest information contained in your communications. They will be your best advocates and can help spread the word about the great work your organization is doing. Of course, not all business decisions will be shared with the entire staff, but you will want to share as much information as possible. This helps your staff stay informed and remain empowered to serve your clients and the community.

Newsletters

Your agency should have an electronic newsletter for the public and perhaps more targeted newsletters for special groups, like volunteers. The newsletters will address the same successes that you plan to detail in your other communications and also should contain audience-specific information. Perhaps you have several volunteer opportunities coming up in the future, and you could ask for interested parties to contact the coordinator to sign up.

Audit Response

The leader of a nonprofit organization should respond in writing to the external auditor's report. If there are any recommendations proposed by the audit firm, the chief executive should lay out the planned changes to the internal controls or other organizational policies and procedures.

The chief executive should first share this written report with the finance/audit committee and then with the entire board of directors. It is not uncommon for the external audit to result in several recommendations based on the latest accounting pronouncements.

Part 4

Putting Your Ideas to Work

"Service to others is the rent you pay for your room here on Earth."
~Muhammad Ali

---

*A*s mentioned in Chapter 12, it is in your best interest to do a personal assessment of your strengths and to hire dedicated and talented staff members to manage the areas that are not your strong points. My dear friend and colleague, Denita Powell Malvern, is an incredibly accomplished programs director. She has shared her expertise with us in the following section.

Program Planning: A How-To

Programs are the heartbeat and lifeline of any nonprofit organization. Programs and activities should be centered on your organization's mission-specific objectives. Many people believe it is easy to execute a successful event or program; however, it takes a great deal of organization and planning if you want to present the best impression of your nonprofit. More importantly, your programs should be designed to not only attract supporters, but to also keep them engaged on an ongoing basis.

When you and your organization are ready to begin the program planning process you should consider the following:

* What type of program(s) are we planning?
* Is the program directly or indirectly aligned with the organization's mission?
* Who is our audience?
* What are the program objectives, goals, and/or learning outcomes?
* What metrics are needed to determine the effectiveness of the program?

And, the most important question you and your team should ask is: are there any other organizations providing the same type(s) of programs?

Like we discussed previously, it is imperative that you do your homework prior to starting a new organization. You need to research every nonprofit in your metropolitan area (within a 30-mile radius) and find out if there are similar nonprofits providing the same programs and services. If you're lucky, you will have a niche organization that meets a unique need in your community. With the explosive growth in the number of nonprofits in the United States, that scenario is unlikely.

Remember, another viable option for your newly formed organization is to build a strategic partnership with an existing organization—one with similar objectives—rather than going it alone. A collaborative program or campaign event can be a great benefit to you. Joining forces with a partner agency will be advantageous by providing exposure to and awareness of your nonprofit and would also aid in building your credibility within the community. Additionally, it would allow you to connect with a new group of potential supporters and could dramatically reduce your program-related expenses—if you negotiate a fair distribution of program expenses (marketing, printed materials, event set-up, speaker fees, catering, etc.).

Strategic Programming

There are three major categories of nonprofit programs: marketing, development, and education. Many people believe that the marketing and development departments serve as a supporting cast for educational programs; although this is true, it shouldn't stop there. If implemented correctly, your marketing and development staff will be critical in helping to provide programming to sustain the life of your nonprofit.

To stay competitive, your nonprofit must be innovative and creative in developing ways to keep your organization in the forefront of the nonprofit world.

Staff members from the marketing, development, and education departments should work in concert on inter-departmental teams to determine which programs should be implemented and what support is needed from each department. As a new entity, it is recommended that you begin with marketing programs and a combination of development and educational programs.

* **Marketing Programs:** Marketing programs are designed to promote your nonprofit and to increase the public's awareness of your organization. Your marketing department must think of inventive ways to highlight your cause and gain support from the community. Some examples of awareness programs include staffing a booth at a community fair or perhaps a city-wide event where a large segment of your target population is likely to participate. Staff or volunteers at the booth can provide brief one-on-one or small group presentations, communicating the mission of your organization in a fun and engaging way. Many nonprofits are utilizing social media outlets to bring awareness to their organizations. Creating a great online marketing program is yet another way to promote your organization and tap into local, regional, and national markets. Interested in getting buy-in for a new idea or concept for your organization? Develop a Facebook page and ask newly invited friends to vote on their favorite marketing campaign slogan, logo, or iconic emblem.

* **Development Programs:** Development programs are crucial to the sustainability of your nonprofit. Development programs and events are intended primarily for fundraising purposes. Your organization will need a sharp and savvy development person or volunteer team to come up with resourceful ideas to get potential donors interested in supporting your organization. A fun example of a development program would be a charrette (an intensive push to finish a project before a deadline). Using the charrette concept, you can invite a small group of prospective donors to a private dinner meeting where they discuss strategies for helping to raise money for your organization. Of course, the goal is to encourage each attendee to loosen up the checkbook and lead the charge by giving generously.

One of the most popular development programs is the Annual Fund Campaign (more detail is provided in the Development/Fundraising segment of this book). Many nonprofit organizations have an Annual Fund that consists of a donation letter and a pledge card—pretty simple. But, if you utilize the creative power of the marketing and education staff, you might find better ways to spruce up the dusty Annual Fund Campaign and make donors excited to give to your organization.

* **Education/Community Outreach Programs:** Educational programs are an effective way to connect your organization with the constituents in which you seek to serve. Some of the leading nonprofits (Habitat for Humanity, Girl Scouts, American Heart Association, etc.) are known for their educational and outreach programs. For example, many cancer awareness organizations provide classes and workshops to educate the public on new statistics and preventive health strategies.

  Depending on the mission of your organization you will need to determine what type and how many educational and outreach programs are needed. As a new organization, I strongly advise you to start with a small program or event. Develop one or two educational programs that can be managed easily by a single person or small team. Be sure to narrow your scope of programs so that potential participants can understand the purpose for offering the program. If your program objectives are too broad, it may be difficult to execute a successful program and participants may feel confused or disconnected from your mission.

Creating a Successful Program

What determines a successful program? Answering the questions at the beginning of this chapter is only the first step. If you feel you are ready to begin planning your program then there is quite a bit of preparation left to do.

When embarking upon a new program you want to look at the full picture before focusing on smaller pieces of the puzzle. Program planners should create an electronic folder/spreadsheet and a hard file (folder, notebook, etc.) to keep all information related to the program. A program checklist is also a helpful tool in making sure you've included everything. A program checklist should include the following information/questions:

* *How large do you anticipate your audience will be? How many people are you attempting to reach with your program?*

* *What are the take-a-ways for program participants (knowledge, skills, logo items/freebies, resources/referrals, etc.)?*

* *What internal/staff resources will you need to plan and deliver your program(s)?*

✳ *What other staff members or support will you need to implement this program? Who will introduce and close the program? Does the marketing team need to promote the program? Will you need volunteers or interns to assist you in managing the program or resources?*

✳ *Have you created your program budget? Will you be selling tickets to cover your program costs? Who will manage the program budget? What supplies and materials will you need to order? Will you be soliciting vendors to offer their services free of charge?*

✳ *Is this a grant-funded program?*

If so, be sure you are meeting all of the requirements outlined in the grant proposal and be prepared to share program results with the funding organization. It is a boon to receive funding from foundations and corporations and you definitely want to ensure the possibility of future funding, so continually review the agreement and make sure you fulfill the agreement. It is a great idea to identify a staff person (usually your accountant or development coordinator) who will provide a close-out grant summary report of the program that clearly states how the grant funds were used, the program impact, and feedback from program participants.

✳ *Will you need to create any contracts or performance agreements?*

Be sure all program contracts and agreements are written so that the nonprofit is protected from various liability issues. There are a number of sample contracts and agreements on the Internet. It is also a good idea to connect with a colleague in the nonprofit world for advice if you have trouble in this area. Program contracts should be approved and signed by the organization's chief executive or designated appointee.

The checklist above will help you begin thinking about the components of program planning. Of course, depending on the nature of your organization, you may need to add other items to your list or use project management software to aid in keeping track of the program process.

A helpful tip from an expert: keep a running list of program managers, speakers, subject experts, and researchers at other nonprofits that you can contact to help you develop concepts or who can serve as potential speakers. Don't forget to think about past program partners, participants, and speakers as potential resources for assisting you in planning your next program.

Chapter 15

Managing a Volunteer Corps

"When the story of these times gets written, we want it to say that we did all we could, and it was more than anyone could have imagined."

~Bono

Volunteers are a tremendous asset to every nonprofit organization. Many nonprofits rely heavily on volunteer support to aid their organization in a variety of tasks including: operational and administrative projects, program and event assistance, front office duties (answering phones, greeting visitors, sorting mail, calling donors to thank them), and countless other assignments. Many nonprofits operate with a limited staff and budget, so it is easy to think that volunteers will solve your human resource shortage. It is important for new nonprofits to realize that having a volunteer corps can also present another set of management and organizational challenges that need to be addressed before starting this process.

If your nonprofit is ready to build a volunteer program, the chief executive and/or leadership team must determine:

* Does your organization have enough tasks, programs, projects, etc., to justify a need for a volunteer program?

* Does your organization currently have a person on staff that has been trained to work with volunteers? Or will you need to begin the search to hire a new staff person?

❋ What are the budget considerations for creating a volunteer program? What would be the cost of training materials? Will you need to bring in an outside expert to provide volunteer training?

❋ Do you have software to manage volunteers or will you need to invest in volunteer software? Will your current staff need to be trained on the new volunteer software?

You and your leadership team must weigh all of the factors before making such an important decision. Remember, volunteers will serve as ambassadors for your newly formed nonprofit. If you are unable to build a viable volunteer program, your volunteers will definitely voice their opinions of your organization to anyone and everyone that will listen to them.

It takes a strong chief executive to manage a team of full-time and part-time staff. When embarking upon any new initiative, like a volunteer program, your organization should build in three times the administrative support to be successful. Resources and support must come from the executive team, general staff, and the volunteer manager or person assigned to oversee the day-to-day operations of the volunteer program. If your organization is not prepared to lend support to this new initiative you should wait on developing a volunteer program until you have all of your supporting staff and resources in place.

Building a Volunteer Corps: Calling in the Cavalry

Everyone who starts a nonprofit is passionate about their organization. Unfortunately, if that passion does not resonate with potential volunteers, you will not be able to build and maintain a thriving volunteer program. The chief executive and designated staff must be able to clearly and effectively communicate the mission of the organization and garner the support of prospective volunteers. You will find that many people are willing to give a great deal of time and support to an organization with a strong mission. However, if you fail to capture the hearts and minds of potential visitors you will not be able to secure enough people interested in supporting your nonprofit. The executive team and key staff (program, marketing/PR, etc.) should determine which messages are the most compelling for potential volunteers. These messages should be used to develop a presentation with pictures, statistics, and any additional information that will position your nonprofit as an organization that should be championed.

Making the Pitch: Recruiting a Team of Loyal Supporters

There are numerous nonprofits providing wonderful resources to the communities in which they serve. Many people are looking for organizations and causes to support and must choose between multiple viable options. When embarking on the process of recruiting volunteers, you must have an impassioned pitch. No, I am not suggesting that you are a salesperson trying to unload a bunch of goods. However, you are selling an organization and a mission, and you need those potential volunteers to feel strongly about what you are attempting to do with your newly formed nonprofit. Make sure that when you are developing your recruitment pitch, the following questions will be answered:

* The reason the nonprofit exists;
* How the organization positively impacts the community;
* Why volunteers are important to your organization; and
* The benefits/perks that potential volunteers will receive as a result of their service
    * Attendance at private events, gallery tours, educational events
    * Free admission to future events
    * Gift shop discounts

Depending on the nature of your nonprofit there may be more reasons that need to be presented during the recruitment pitch. It is a good idea to enlist the support of your marketing person and any other staff person that will need assistance from volunteers. Since the volunteer program will add another component to your nonprofit, it is a good idea for staff members to feel connected to this new initiative and help support its future success. Getting the entire staff involved in the volunteer recruitment process reinforces the administrative support needed to build and maintain a successful volunteer program.

Although you will likely designate a staff member to be responsible for volunteer management, every staff member must be available to the volunteer coordinator and volunteers when needed. Employees should also assist in writing volunteer job descriptions, providing brief recruitment presentations, and helping to develop the recruitment pitch for potential volunteers.

Now that you've developed your pitch, you're ready to share it with the world, right? Not so fast! To be fully prepared, you must also think about your recruitment strategy. Who should you recruit? And from where? Recruiting volunteers for your nonprofit organization can be just as important as hiring your paid staff. Depending on the nature of your nonprofit, you may want to consider partnering with similar organizations to find out where to publicize your need for volunteers. For example, if you provide services for senior citizens, you may want to create a database of area nursing homes, senior day care facilities, and companies that provide services for seniors. After creating your database you may want to send volunteer recruitment flyers to the employees of these facilities and companies. Similarly, if your nonprofit organization provides tutoring services to special needs children, you may want to send recruitment information to teachers, area schools, or you may even place a small, inexpensive add in a school trade publication. Of course, no matter what your mission or service you can reach a great deal of people if you incorporate social media into your recruitment campaign.

Local schools are ripe for potential volunteers. There are many high school and college students that need community service hours as part of their graduation requirements. Your staff should send recruitment flyers to school counselors and administrators for approval. If allowed, you might even consider providing a presentation to students about your nonprofit and the need for dedicated volunteers.

Ultimately, it is up to you and your staff to be creative when thinking of ways to recruit prospective volunteers and the organizations and institutions that can provide you with access to hundreds and sometimes thousands of future supporters. Keep in mind that many corporations also seek volunteer engagement opportunities for their employees. If your nonprofit has corporate donors, be sure to connect with the HR staff to inquire about giving a presentation to employees. If your organization provides services to a specific gender or ethnic group, find out if those companies have affinity groups that you can connect with in order to develop program and volunteer partnership opportunities. Your board members will likely have some great ideas for partnerships that will connect your organization with potential volunteers.

The Application & Selection Process

Now that you have your recruitment strategy in place you must be sure that you have the internal infrastructure in place to take potential volunteers through the application and training process. The application process should be simple and easy for your potential volunteers. If the process is too cumbersome or time intensive to complete, be prepared to lose some of your newly identified recruits. During the recruitment process, it is a good idea to include a brief checklist or overview of all of the steps needed to become a volunteer. Also, be sure to cover your organization's application and selection process during the recruitment session.

Volunteer Application

The leadership team must determine what information to include on the volunteer application. At a minimum, you want to include general information on the prospective volunteer (name, phone, address, e-mail, etc.); the days/hours the person is available to volunteer; areas of volunteer interest (administration, programming, general office, marketing, events, etc.); office skills and certifications; and any additional information that may be decided upon by your organization. If your nonprofit needs to create a volunteer application, there are a number of sample volunteer forms available for download on the Internet. Your organization should utilize both a paper application (available at your organization) and an electronic application (that can be accessed from your website, emailed to prospective volunteers, or you could also provide a link on your social media sites). You want to give potential volunteers as many options as possible to submit their application and begin the volunteer selection process for your organization.

Selection Process

Every nonprofit is different and one organization's requirements may be vastly different from another one. For example, if your organization provides services for children it is important that your volunteers complete a background check to ensure that they do not have a criminal background, especially crimes of abuse or issues involving children. If your organization requires that volunteers deal with petty cash or valuable items, a background check can assure you that a potential volunteer does not have a criminal record involving theft. There are some situations that should not be up for review or debate. Your organization must set clear guidelines on what factors or issues will make a person ineligible for volunteer service with your nonprofit. There may be rare instances when your organization will need to be flexible when selecting potential volunteers and you may need to select volunteers on a case by case basis. Whatever policy you set in place for your organization be sure to be fair and consistent to avoid potential accusations of discrimination and/or unfair treatment.

During your selection process you may also want to consider what purpose the volunteer will fill for your organization. Will you recruit all eligible volunteers that meet your defined criteria? Will you select volunteers based on a certain skill set or background? Will you accept volunteers year-round or at certain times during a year? Again, whatever policy is established by your organization must be clearly communicated, posted, and followed by every person involved with the volunteer management process.

Maintaining the Volunteer Program

Congratulations! You've recruited your volunteers and are well on your way to maintaining a thriving volunteer program. Your staff members are supportive, your volunteer manager is an organizational genius, and you have successfully incorporated an additional core of unpaid staff ready to help you fulfill your organization's mission.

Although this lofty success deserves a round of applause, keep in mind that you did a lot of work to recruit and build your volunteer corps and now you have to work just as hard to keep them. Earlier in the chapter we discussed the need to have three times the staff support to have a successful volunteer program. In these next few sections you will understand why this is so critical.

Volunteers, like paid staff, need on-going training and resources to continue to be an asset to you and your nonprofit. In addition, keep in mind that your volunteers have needs and over time will appreciate being given tools and resources that can help them thrive within and outside of your organization. To effectively maintain your volunteer program your organization must manage three key volunteer areas: volunteer training, volunteer communication, and incentives.

The Anatomy of a Volunteer

You have recruited a nice pool of volunteers that are eager to help you fulfill your organization's mission and objectives. Congratulations! Now, what are your expectations for the dedicated and talented volunteers?

A successful volunteer program *must* begin with a strong training component. When developing your training materials and presentation notes, it is important to remember that there is an anatomy to volunteers. Your new volunteers have a unique make-up, a diverse composition that must be taken seriously. Training tools and resources should be created with the following considerations in mind:

* **Volunteers should be assigned tasks based on their interests and skill set.** Training materials should be developed and presented in a way to help potential volunteers understand that there are specific duties that need to be completed within your organization.

* **More than 50% of volunteers donate their time to other nonprofit organizations.** It is important to have a structured program that will keep volunteers engaged. Many volunteers enjoy learning new things and developing new skills. A poorly executed training process will deter volunteers from remaining with your organization since they have other options to choose from.

* **Volunteers want to feel as if they are making a difference.** It is important to remember that volunteers are stakeholders in your nonprofit. Volunteers should be given an opportunity to read and hear about the successes of your organization and to see, first hand, how their service has helped advance your mission. Perhaps you can include a volunteer story or service statistics on your website, through a social media campaign, or in your organization's annual report. Perhaps you can get a local news writer to do a special interest story on one or two of your active volunteers. Your volunteer manager must find as many creative ways as possible to show volunteers that your organization could not function as effectively without their continued service.

* **Volunteers want to be valued and recognized as a critical part of your organization.** It is important to think of volunteers as unpaid staff. During the training process, it is important for the volunteer coordinator or trainer to highlight the benefits available to volunteers of your organization.

❋ **The Volunteer Corps is made up of a group of diverse individuals with varying personalities, needs, and motivators.** The training materials and presentations must provide a detailed overview of the nonprofit's policies and procedures. Volunteers should be asked to sign a document that they agree to abide by the rules and guidelines of your organization. By creating a standard of procedures to follow, no one can say that you are showing partiality or engaging in any discriminatory behavior. Most volunteers will be great and easy to direct. Unfortunately, there are a small percentage of volunteers that will challenge your staff and may break a rule or two. Volunteer and nonprofit staff must be willing to enforce the policies and be consistent when dealing with all of their volunteers. As you will recall from Tina McIntosh's advice from the Joy's House case study, not all volunteers will be a fit for your organization. You should be prepared to have a candid, straight-forward conversation with a volunteer that should be excused from service.

The above-mentioned training tips are recommendations and should be incorporated by your training team. Of course, the training process should be customized to fit the individual needs of your nonprofit organization.

Volunteer Training

Volunteer training can cover a wide variety of topics ranging from customer service, software and skill-building, mission-sharing techniques, survey collection, and the list goes on and on. Volunteers love training because it is another indicator that your organization values its volunteer corps. In addition, it provides volunteers with an opportunity to develop, build, or enhance upon a current or desired skill. Volunteer training programs can be as simple as asking your marketing staff to provide a presentation on your organization's brand and mission. It might include a data entry training workshop from your development team on how to use development software (e.g., Raiser's Edge/Blackbaud, etc.). Or, it might include an outside motivational speaker or customer service professional. When creating your volunteer training options you want to be sure to keep your overall budget in mind. While there will be some costs associated with volunteer trainings your goal is to get as many donated services, tools, and resources as possible. As a nonprofit you want to be strategic in bargaining with other nonprofits on services and resources. Perhaps you and a partnering nonprofit will provide a joint training program, sharing the costs of the expert speaker.

* **Determining the frequency of volunteer trainings:** Your volunteer coordinator and supporting staff will need to determine how often volunteer trainings will be scheduled (annually, quarterly, project basis). When possible it is best for the volunteer training schedule to be set months in advance. Ideally, the volunteer staff should work with the executive team on what trainings are needed. Volunteers should be given ample notice on volunteer schedules, topics, and dates. In rare instances, volunteers may be given an opportunity to take classes that will require them to pay a small fee (for example, CPR certification). Be sure that volunteers are aware that these paid courses will be beneficial and make sure to give them time to secure funds. Your nonprofit may also want to negotiate a discounted rate for large groups of volunteers interested in paid training courses.

* **Training materials:** Training materials are an important piece of the training program. You will find that people have different learning styles and it is important to develop materials that will help the visual and auditory learner. When developing training materials in written form be sure to provide a presentation or auditory component that helps to reinforce the learning (where possible). In some instances, there may be a YouTube video or instructional DVD that can be shared with the training group. It is important to have a clear budget for training materials for all of your training sessions, so that you can manage the expenditures. To keep costs low, you may want to provide PDF files for volunteers to download and bring with them to the training sessions.

* **Peer-to-peer training:** Some of your volunteers learn kinesthetically and need hands-on training. It is a great idea to partner senior/skilled volunteers with new or untrained volunteers. Peer-to-peer training gives the new volunteers additional support, builds camaraderie among volunteers, and it gives your senior volunteers a chance to assume a training/supervisory role. When creating a peer-to-peer training scenario it is important for the volunteer staff to provide the proper oversight and guidance to make sure this training technique is a success. The volunteer staff should also monitor the interaction between peer training partners to ensure it is a good fit for both volunteers.

Volunteer Communication

Your organization may have great plans for volunteers; however, if they aren't effectively communicated it won't matter. Volunteers need clear, concise, and systematic correspondence to maintain a strong level of engagement. The volunteer coordinator must be extremely organized and detail-oriented in capturing the skills, needs, and profile of each volunteer in your organization.

* **Volunteer database management:** The volunteer staff should be able to keep accurate files for every volunteer associated with your nonprofit including: postal mail and e-mail address, volunteer hours, completed trainings, skills, interests, etc. It is rare, but if a volunteer decides to discontinue working with your organization it is important that the database reflect this information as well. You never want to find yourself in a situation where a former volunteer is contacted for a volunteer project after they have discontinued service. It will make your volunteer staff appear disorganized and unprofessional.

* **Project management:** A comprehensive volunteer database can also be used to manage your projects. The volunteer coordinator can work with your staff members to identify key volunteers with specific skill sets and expertise needed to assist in various projects.

* **Website, newsletters, and phone calls:** In an ideal world every volunteer would have access to the Internet and e-mail. Unfortunately, this is not always the case. Your volunteer staff must be prepared to communicate with your volunteers based on the communication methods available to your volunteer corps. The good news is that 80 percent of your volunteers will be able to access the Internet to retrieve information. For this group of volunteers, it is important to leave information about volunteer trainings, volunteer opportunities, and other pertinent information in the volunteer section of your website or in an e-mail document/newsletter. For the 20 percent of your volunteers without Internet access you will need to make personal phone calls and send out mailings with volunteer updates and pertinent information. Be sure to use your volunteer database to keep track of information sharing and who has not responded to volunteer correspondence. In many cases, your volunteer coordinator will need to be a master in the art of follow-up when it comes to securing volunteers for projects and assignments.

* **Conflict resolution:** When dealing with a large group of people with different personalities, opinions, and motivators, conflicts are sure to arise from time to time. Potential conflicts may involve a volunteer and a member of the public, two volunteers, a volunteer and a staff member. Your volunteer staff should be trained in some form of conflict resolution in order to be comfortable dealing with difficult and sensitive issues. There should be a clear conflict resolution policy/statement provided to each volunteer

during their training process. Of course, the goal of conflict resolution is to de-escalate the situation and get all parties involved to find a peaceable solution to the issue. In rare instances, some situations may result in a volunteer resigning from volunteer service or your organization may be forced to excuse a volunteer from service. No matter the situation, you want to remain respectful and professional to avoid any further backlash or fallout from the situation.

* **Policy and procedure enforcement:** Policy and procedural enforcement is one of the best ways to reduce conflict and difficult situations. Volunteers should be given a complete list of your organization's policies and procedures to follow. If there is ever an instance where a volunteer has broken a policy or procedure, there needs to be a clear set of corrective actions. The volunteer coordinator should work with the organization's human resources specialist and the executive leadership team to create a disciplinary policy for volunteers.

* **Feedback and evaluation:** Feedback from volunteers is very important and should be considered a valuable source of information. Volunteers are a unique group of people because they share their thoughts and opinions with nothing to lose. Volunteers have the distinctive position of being a part of your organization, but can also view your nonprofit from the sidelines. Volunteers are usually very vocal about policies, procedures, programs, events, and a host of other topics. Volunteers are also a great test group for new ideas and initiatives. When you rely upon volunteers for their feedback and opinions, you will be satisfying their need to feel valued and accepted by you and your organization.

Volunteer Incentive Program

While many people volunteer for the mere joy of knowing that they have made a difference, a few extra perks are always nice—really nice! Every nonprofit needs *free* human resources and since many volunteers donate their time to other institutions it is in your best interest to stay competitive. A volunteer incentive program can be used as a recruitment tool and/or a way to keep your volunteers connected to your organization.

* **Volunteer appreciation:** It is always nice to feel appreciated and your volunteers need to be treated as valued members of your team and appreciated for helping you reach your organizational goals. Volunteer appreciations can be implemented in a number of ways including: an appreciation reception, luncheon, or dinner where the volunteers are recognized, honored,

and given a small token of appreciation; volunteer service awards; or a special mention in your organization's annual fund for the volunteer(s) of the year for the most service hours given for the fiscal year. The type of volunteer appreciation you give will be determined by your organization's budget and your staff's creativity.

* **A discount, free perks, etc.:** Freebies and perks are also a great way to honor your volunteers. Consider working with your staff members on providing discounted or free program admissions to volunteers and their guests, free memberships, or parking privileges. Perhaps you can provide a discount on a service from a partner organization. Your perks and volunteer benefits can be set up on a tier program where certain perks are provided to volunteers who have provided one, two, five, or ten years of service to your organization. Be sure to post the incentive programs so that volunteers will have something to work toward and look forward to receiving.

Sending Out the Troops: Volunteers Ready to Serve

Your volunteer program is a direct reflection of you, your staff, and most importantly, your mission. The success of your volunteer program is contingent upon how well you've trained your volunteer corps on your mission and the role they will play in executing your stated goals.

Your volunteer program—be it simple or complex—must be an integral part of your organization's structure. As a nonprofit, you will need to be creative in utilizing the skills of your volunteer corps. In addition, you must be willing and eager to reward them for their dedication in helping your nonprofit make a positive impact in your community.

Chapter 16

Assessing Your Programs: What Does the Public Really Think?

"So, take what's inside you and make big, bold choices.
And for those who can't speak for themselves, use bold voices.
And make friends and love well, bring art to this place.
And make this world better for the whole human race."

~Jamie Lee Curtis

In Chapter 14 the question was raised, *how can you determine your program's success?* The answer can be found in the feedback from your program participants. There are quite a few reputable audience research companies that provide assessment services to nonprofits. Unfortunately, newly formed organizations may feel that in order to evaluate their programs they need to invest a small fortune in a consulting firm that will help them in the evaluation process. The reality is, every nonprofit can begin assessing the effectiveness of its programs. In fact, there are several easy and effective ways to find out what program participants and supporters think of your organization.

Direct Feedback

Of course, the quickest form of feedback you will receive is direct engagement with participants. Ask people a direct question, *so what did you think of the program?* Believe me; people are very interested in providing feedback if it will help improve upon an area. Others may need to vent about their experience. If a program participant had a bad experience with your organization it is in your best interest to address the concern(s) as soon as possible. A disappointed program participant will share her unpleasant experience with more people than the person who enjoyed your program offering(s).

Comment Cards

Comment cards are a quick and simple way to receive feedback from program participants. If written anonymously, more people may be willing to provide their candid opinions of your nonprofit and the programs you offer. Comment cards are the easiest way to capture a visitor's true feelings and impressions of your nonprofit. Every nonprofit has a different approach to comment cards. You and your staff can have index cards with pencils available for people to record their thoughts about anything related to your nonprofit. By keeping the cards blank you will allow the person freedom to write anything that is important to them as it relates to their experiences with your nonprofit. If you are interested in a particular area of your nonprofit you can list one or two questions on a comment card. This option allows you to get feedback on a program or service that may be new to your nonprofit or any specific areas of concern. If your nonprofit agrees to use this option it is important to leave a space for program participants to leave any "additional comments" that he or she may have to share with your organization.

Survey Forms

Survey forms can be easy or complex depending on their purpose for your organization. Survey forms are a more formal alternative to the informal comment card mentioned above. Many people shy away from completing survey forms because they seem to be too long and time consuming. Your nonprofit must be sure to keep the survey forms brief so that you will increase the number of people that will complete them. When formulating your questions be sure to include feedback from your marketing, program, and development departments. All three areas have specific stakeholders and need survey data to help them in their respective roles. Key information that should be included in every survey form is demographic data. This information may include ethnicity, age, gender, zip code, household income, etc. While this data is important to your organization, regretfully, some people may opt out of completing this section because they feel that it is too personal. Where possible, it is recommended that staff members or volunteers distribute survey forms to supporters and/or program participants. Volunteers and staff members can stress to survey participants that completing the survey form will help the organization fulfill its mission, develop better programs, and raise more money. Of course, a soft sell is a great way to improve on the number of complete survey forms that you will receive. If your organization needs survey data to share with a potential or existing donor then you may want to include some funds from your budget to include a small incentive for individuals that take the time to complete the survey form in its entirety.

Online Feedback

Online feedback is a great audience evaluation technique that can be incorporated into your organization's social media campaign. It is no secret that marketing and advertising your nonprofit can be very expensive. So, why not use social media outlets like Twitter, YouTube, and Facebook to bring additional exposure to your nonprofit and gauge how well your supporters and followers understand the mission of your organization and the programs you offer. Your organization needs to have a savvy person on staff that is able to connect with your supporters and followers and get them to respond to your questions. It is also a great way to promote your organization and provide an opportunity for online giving.

Another recommendation is for your nonprofit to utilize an online survey tool that is easy to navigate and from which you can retrieve survey data. A very popular online resource is SurveyMonkey, although I'm sure there are other comparable online programs. An online survey tool will allow you to create your questions, build the survey tool, and send the link to your supporters, members, donors, community stakeholders, and the general public. The greatest benefit of using a survey tool is that it can process and analyze the data for you. If you do not have a statistician or a person on staff that has been trained in data entry and analysis, a survey tool can be your best friend. A survey tool can provide statistical information with percentages, numbers, and anecdotal data that can be used by your organization to aid in grant writing, annual reporting, marketing, and program development.

Focus Groups

Focus groups can serve many purposes for your nonprofit. Initially, participants in your focus group can be used to determine how well you are accomplishing your mission, presenting your programs, and marketing your nonprofit's brand. But the role of a focus group shouldn't stop there. Focus groups can also be used to gauge excitement and interest in a new program, or a new marketing or development campaign. In essence, a focus group can be used to test any new service or program you wish to introduce to your audience. Once your test group has completed their participation in the focus group you now have a group of community stakeholders that can share your current and future plans with other like-minded individuals who will hopefully support your nonprofit. So, a focus group can also provide your organization with free PR if you are strategic in structuring the content and direction of the focus group. Remember to make good use of the time you have with the group because they have chosen to participate in your focus group out of a vested interest in your organization or their curiosity about the role your organization intends to play in your community.

It's a Wrap

Whether you are developing a marketing, development, or educational program, the evaluation component is a key step in the program planning process that cannot be ignored. Many nonprofits' programs are destined to fail because they neglected to plan effectively on the front end. Remember that your organization has been created to meet a need or provide a resource/service for the community. It is important for your organization to stay connected with the public, your supporters, and donors to remain relevant. Yes, it is important to capture feedback from your constituents; but, you should also find a way to incorporate their thoughts and recommendations into your operational plan. If your supporters know that you have listened to and implemented their recommendations they will feel like a vested partner in your nonprofit and will likely become a devoted supporter of your organization.

However, if your organization fails to see the value in community feedback it will likely lose its standing and significance in the community. Even worse, your organization may run the risk of only being relevant in the minds of those closest to the mission and operations. If this happens, it may be a tremendous challenge for you and your staff to change the community's perception of your nonprofit.

Part 5
Funding Your Work

Chapter 17

Designing a Sustainable Funding Plan

"It is our collective and individual responsibility to protect and nurture the global family, to support its weaker members, and to preserve and tend to the environment in which we all live."

~The Dalai Lama

---

*T*his chapter is a contribution from my close friend and colleague, Fran Lobpries, CFRE. Trust me; never underestimate the value of the expertise that a seasoned and dedicated fundraising professional can add to your organizational foundation.

Integrated Resource Development

A True/False Quiz

It is very tempting to think that because you have created an organization to do good work or provide a much needed service, donors will be lining up to give you their money. This myth is further propagated by the fact that many foundations, government grants, and major donors are infatuated with the "new." A new solution, a new idea, a fresh approach, while excellent in concept, often fades when faced with the realities of the funders' marketplace.

Donations are not free. Donations are a social contract. Donations are an exchange of money for a social action in the community to solve a problem… to accomplish your stated mission, project, program, proposal, or building. When you or a representative of your nonprofit accepts a donation for a stated purpose, you have made a contract. You may or may not go to prison for not keeping up your end of the bargain, but your reputation, earned or unearned in the marketplace, will be just one of the factors affecting donations.

Big funders like new, but they also like to be sure about their investments. From the donors' perspective, a gift or grant is an investment. Their pre-grant questions (read: demands) of you are calculated to determine their investment's risk. Established organizations have stood the test of time and are, therefore, more trusted investments. The same funding sources that like new are also quick to add, "we do not do operational expenses (read: your salary)." Therefore, you will need a cadre of supporters willing to fund the basics before approaching most foundations. Big money gifts are wonderful when you get them, but do not plan your budget around them. It is likely they will not come every year.

You can offset some of your donor's fears by taking the steps discussed in the previous chapters such as recruiting a diversified, well-connected, strong board; forging brilliant collaborations; and maintaining transparently clean financials.

In this chapter, we will answer the question of how to gain donor support for your good work. First, let's check out a few falsehoods that can derail your funding efforts.

False-isms

* **Falsehood #1:** Very often, board members and non-development professionals jump to the conclusion that we need to have a special event or send out direct mail to raise money. Why? Because those are the fundraising experiences with which we are most familiar. Who doesn't receive a mountain of unsolicited mail and invitations from charities you barely or absolutely have never heard from before? You may be thinking, "It must be working. Look at how many charities are doing it." Yes, direct mail and special events do have their place in an integrated resource development plan; just not yet.

❋ **Falsehood #2:** We can hire a development director and he/she will go to their contacts for the money. Yes, a professional fundraiser (I do recommend a Certified Fund Raising Executive [CFRE]) can set you on a good path, implement the "right" strategies, and raise support for the mission. But, it is against the Association of Fundraising Professional's code of ethics "to take donors with us." The work one does for one organization belongs to that organization. The next organization receives the benefit of the fundraiser's prior experience and knowledge of donors in the community who are interested in a certain type of charity. It is certainly acceptable to send announcement cards to those previous donors with whom fundraisers have a personal relationship. However, it is not acceptable to take an organization's database of donors with you to another organization!

Raising money may be a staff-driven function; but, it is not a solo job. Without dedicated well-connected business, professional, and community social leaders, your nonprofit will be swimming upstream and not making a lot of headway.

❋ **Falsehood #3:** "Our work in the community speaks for itself." This is RARELY the case. Most good work is behind the scenes, out of the spotlight, and for very good reasons. It is to protect those that are being helped. Communicating how you have helped and what a difference it has made, is fundamental to the case to give. Without a definitive method of measuring progress and telling the stories of change, donors will not know or be convinced of your organization's legitimate function.

Truisms Please?

❋ **Truism #1:** Not all development is gifts/grants. How much can you charge for your services? Will you make money on some and give discounts or free services to others? What is the gap between your income and expenses if you giveaway your goal number of services this year? This should be worked out in your business plan; but, if not, do it now.

- The gap will be the primary responsibility of the strategic fund raising plan. It should be reflected in the budget. It should be approved by the board, but not without first asking your development team what they can reasonably project to raise in the coming year and how much that effort will cost. I find it amazing how often the finance team and the program team make a determination of what they will do for the next year without including the development team.

- The best results will come from an open forum addressing: the availability of capable and willing volunteer leadership; the strength of the program to make an effectual reportable change; the strength of financial reserves to allow for the risk of new strategies; the donors' history; strategies; and the volunteer and staff resources of the development department.

⁂ **Truism #2:** Communications and marketing are critical to the success of the development plan (i.e., if marketing for the products made by disabled adults is designed to position those products as the best available rather than meticulously crafted by disabled citizens, the market is unaware of the mission and service to the community, thereby weakening market readiness to respond to requests to give). All communication and marketing should be in close alignment with the strategic plan and the resource development plan. Conversely, when advertising your special event or any other fundraising communications, it is critical that brand, slogan, colors, and logos are all consistent with marketing.

Integration of communications, marketing, and programming is usually so simple in the beginning when an organization is small. However, with each new employee, the more important an organizationally integrated written communication and revenue development plan becomes. Next is a SMART plan to help you design your own.

Plan Your Work.
Work Your Plan.
Repeat.

Building a SMART Resource Development Plan:
Like for-profit organizations, nonprofits must have a detailed board-approved resource development plan if money sources are to feel confident enough to invest. An integrated resource development plan begins with the strategic plan giving a consistent overarching base for the goals of the organization.

Step #1: Not all fund-raising is about the money. As I prepare a strategic development plan for an organization, I first look at what it will need from the organization before it can reach outside its inner circle of friends. Number one on

(continued)

Plan Your Work. Work Your Plan. Repeat. (continued)

my list is 100% giving by the board and staff...with a minimum set for the board and a goal, such as one hour of pay, set for staff.

Non-Monetary Strategies for Development
EXAMPLE:

- Implement a plan for ongoing recruitment/training of fundraising volunteers. Recruit a minimum of twenty (20) non-board volunteers to work in fund development

- Board Chairs develop committees outside of board to accomplish objectives

- Develop new prospects for personal solicitation, campaign, and direct mail solicitation; cultivate family foundations/trusts

- Strengthen Major Donor program, board and staff understanding of the purpose and process of cultivation, solicitation, stewardship

Step #2: Your monetary fundraising goals are predicated on the negotiated budget and the viability of your constituency base. Stay high level with these strategies. Your income projections will be based on your history and vision. Your development SMART plan will help you make realistic projections.

A sample matrix is shown below. It can be tailored to fit your organization's particular goals.

Monetary Fundraising Goals
Sample

Annual Fund Budget by Constituency	FY2010 Actual Income	FY 2011 Actual Income	FY 2012 Income Projections	% Increase 2011 to 2012
Individuals	$46,132	$30,406	$81,000	166%
Major Donors	$15,000	$15,200	$32,000	110%
Foundations/Corporations	$48,825	$71,525	$120,000	68%
Churches/Organizations	$1,801	$1,384	$20,000	1,345%
Special Events	$12,524	$65,521	$216,000	230%
Other (Unsolicited Income)	$1,009	$15,768	$0	0%
TOTAL Donated INCOME	$125,291	$199,804	$468,000	134%

(continued)

Plan Your Work. Work Your Plan. Repeat. (continued)

If you have identified five types of constituents, then write at least five (5) SMART Goals.

What is a SMART Goal? Define the SMART of each strategy:

- Strategic (relates directly to mandate of strategic plan);
- Measurable (defines how you and your donors will know if you accomplished your goal);
- Accountable (who is responsible for tracking and reaching the goal);
- Realistic (what factors and methods are you basing your goals);
- Timeline (when will the strategy be accomplished as well as the major milestones)

Sample Organization's Strategic Plan: If the organization's strategic plan calls for a 50% growth in services to meet the verifiable community need for day-care to low-income parents over the next five years, our fundraising strategy to meet the goal might be to raise 10% each year for five years.

Sample Development Plan Goal:

> **Strategy 1:** Board member and staff increased participation in giving, sharing stories, and serving on committee/projects
>
> > **Measurable:** Increase donations 10% with 100% participation in giving and serving
> >
> > **Accountable:** Board Chair assisted by Development Chair
> >
> > **Realistic:** 87% board donations, 50% serving in prior year
> >
> > **Timely:** Donation pledges and committee agreements signed in first quarter; service throughout year

Step #3: As with the board example above, continue building your resource plan based on your constituents: individuals, foundations, government, corporations, organizations, and special events. Build method plans for approaching each of the above constituents using experienced development professional's advice or consultation. Typically, the plan is built on constituent history, market opportunities, and organizational resources.

(continued)

Plan Your Work. Work Your Plan. Repeat. (continued)

SAMPLE Special Event Strategy:

> **STRATEGY:** Foundation grants
>
> **MEASURABLE GOAL:** $50,000; 24 foundation proposals; 12 reports; at least 10 new foundation prospects
>
> **ACCOUNTABILITY:** Board Chair, Development Director
>
> **REALISTIC METHOD:** Three proposals submitted in last quarter of 2011; 81 foundations identified as 2012 prospects
>
> **TIME FRAME:** Ongoing throughout the year—see grant calendar

As a new organization, experienced development professionals, and community leaders' assessments of your plan will be helpful in meeting the "realistic requirement." It will be in your organization's best interest to listen and consider all of the free advice you will receive. As you gain traction, it will be easier to decide which recommendations should be acted upon.

Methods for Acquiring Money

You are aware that a diversified portfolio of stocks provides a safety net for your investments. When one stock is good another may be down, but your portfolio's value keeps chugging along...at least in theory. The same theory applies to creating a balanced development plan.

Do not put all your eggs in one basket when it comes to raising money. Your plan should involve a number of different methods, reaching out to different constituents, at different times of the year.

If your target market of donors is primarily "twenty-somethings," then obviously your social media, text-to-give, and special event programs will be a large part of your development portfolio. Conversely, if you are raising money from seniors 65 and over, planned giving, direct mail, and major donor calls may fill your calendar.

Using the SMART strategies, build the development work plan based on the METHODS outlined to meet each strategic goal (i.e., golf tournament, annual fund mailing, and text-to-give program). Breaking down each method using the SMART process, you will begin to understand what it will take to make the budget/plan numbers become your reality.

Build the income and expense budget for each method. Compare expected net income with the organization's defined program needs. Let the negotiating begin. Please do include the development team as you determine your dollar goals.

Sample Revenue Projection by Activity

Resources by Activity	FY2010 Actual Income	FY 2011 Actual Income	FY 2012 Income Projections	% Increase 2011 to 2012
Board & Staff	$14,153	$14,099	$30,000	113%
School Donations	$6,669	$4,790	$5,000	4%
Site Donations	$7,210	$5,512	$6,000	9%
Text-to-Give	$0	$0	$10,000	100%
"Friends"—Volunteer program	$15,929	$5,344	$10,000	87%
Honorarium/Memorial Gifts (over 5k)	$2,171	$662	$2,000	202%
Major Donor Program	$15,000	$15,200	$50,000	229%
Newsletter	$1,000	$0	$0	0%
Miscellaneous	$1,009	$15,767	$0	0%
Individual Total	**$63,141**	**$46,373**	**$112,000**	**143%**
Foundations Grant Calendar (includes capital improvements)	$18,825	$22,025	$50,000	127%
Corporate Non-Event	$0	$0	$10,000	100%
State Grant	$30,000	$49,500	$60,000	21%
Educational Organizations	$1,801	$1,384	$20,000	1,345%
Organizations Total	**$50,626**	**$72,909**	**$140,000**	**92%**
Raffles	$8,147	$8,426	$100,000	1,086%
Special Events Total	**$11,524**	**$65,521**	**$216,000**	**230**
TOTAL INCOME	**$125,291**	**$199,804**	**$468,000**	**134%**

For an example, one of our special event methods is to host a second annual golf tournament. (You know that you cannot call it an annual anything until you are in the second year.) Below you will see the SMART plan for the golf tournament. This is enough of a plan for budgeting and recruiting of the leadership; however, please continue planning and defining each step of the event in tremendous detail. Why so much detail? You do not want to start all over every year do you? With a good plan that clearly defines the jobs to be done and who will be responsible for each as well as a detailed wrap up session, you will be able to improve your process each year.

Golf Tournament SMART Plan

METHOD STRATEGY: Golf tournament to engage 10% more corporations and increase 1k donors by 10%

- **MEASURABLE GOALS:** 144 Golfers; 26 Sponsors; $100,000 gross/ $70,800 net

- **ACCOUNTABILITY:** (Golf Chair: Name) (Golf Co-Chairs: Names); Development Director; Committee Members: (Names)

- **REALISTIC METHOD:** Committee recruitment in January; sponsor packets out to last year's sponsors in February; committee list of new sponsors out in March; sponsor follow-up calls by May. Player recruitment June–September. October thank you and clean up. (FY2011 grossed $50,000 with late start beginning in August)

- **TIME FRAME:** January–October 2012

In this example, approximately 30 percent of the gross will be eaten up in expenses. Actually, this is a good "return on investment" (ROI) for a special event. Average special event ROI can be 50 percent or less. Often, events prove to be a lot of work for a little money.

Special events should be used to accomplish a number of important objectives:

✳ **Visibility in the community.** Events can be wonderful opportunities to share your story with new prospective donors or to have your organization recognized in the media. The real rate of return is gauged on how many, for how much, of those who attend are still on your donor list one year later. Did you have good follow-up and methods for engaging new donors after the event?

* **Credibility through alliances.** When you have a superstar endorsing your event and sharing that star power with your constituents and would-be donors, you can increase your donor worthiness as a result. (And, the telethon was born!)

* **Face-to-face time.** Everyone's time is precious. When you have several hours of a potential donor's attention, use it wisely. Plan carefully who will host each potential donor. What will the talking points be? What is the program's take-away? Did you demonstrate the importance of what you do? Or, did you just have fun?

* **Make money.** Okay, yes that happens...sometimes. But, it is not a slam-dunk, especially if it is your first one or weather is a factor. The "friend-raising" opportunities far outweigh the fundraising for the majority. Consider the huge amount of hours of staff and volunteer time and money that go into creating an event.

Was it worth it? To me the most important reason to have an event is so, as a fundraiser, I can tell our story, gauge interest level, and ask people to participate in the area that best matches the donors' interest. This goes for board members, other staff, and volunteers who are savvy enough to engage attendees.

Timing Is Everything

A grant turned in after the deadline is several weeks of wasted staff time (and money). An end-of-the-year direct mail campaign not mailed until January is lost revenue. How do you make sure all the methods are completed at just the right time? Calendars.

When the development plan and goals are approved, build a calendar, for each method, using the timelines established in the SMART plan.

SAMPLE Activity Calendar

Activity	January	February	March	April	May	June
Individual Board Solicitation	Board Retreat— Dev Plan agreement	Pledge Cards completed	Report progress back to board	Follow up individually with unpledged	Help those seeking donations (give or get)	Continue monitoring and assisting all board to be successful
Major Gift Prospecting, Cultivation, Soliciting, Stewarding	Minimum of 3 contacts per week throughout the year by Dev Director	Minimum of 3 contacts per quarter for board members	1st small group home party hosted by advisory board	Follow up visits to new prospects from party	Minimum of 3 contacts per week throughout the year by Dev Director	Minimum of 3 contacts per quarter for board members
Donor Acquisition	Capture emails	Monthly online news story	Quarterly newsletter to mail; Spring house party	Ball game event invitations and request to give	Raffle exposure	Raffle exposure; Quarterly Newsletter

Build an accountability calendar for each person/committee named as a responsible party for a strategy. A sample accountability calendar appears next.

Sample Accountability Calendar

Accountability	January	February	March	April	May
Board Chair	Lead Board Retreat; Solicit board members; Major Gift Calls as needed; Approve and sign Grant applications	Board Pledge Cards completed; Recruit Chairs; Major Gift Calls as needed; Approve and sign Grant applications	Article in Newsletter; Major Gift Calls as needed; Approve and sign Grant applications	Follow up individually with unpledged board members; Major Gift Calls as needed; Approve and sign Grant applications	Help those seeking donations (give or get); Major Gift Calls as needed; Approve and sign Grant applications
Development Chair	**Minimum of 3 Major Gift contacts per week; Grant calendar requirements; **Create Golf Sponsor Package	Distribute Golf Packages; Make follow-up calls to sponsors; facilitate committee	1st small group home party hosted by advisory board	Follow up visits to new prospects from party	Minimum of 3 contacts per week throughout the year by Dev Director

(continued)

Sample Accountability Calendar (continued)

Accountability	January	February	March	April	May
Golf Committee Chair	*Recruit Committee and meet; Reserve Course for date and time; Determine sponsor benefits*	*Approve package; Ask committee to find sponsors*	*2nd round of sponsor packages; Make Sponsor calls*	*Make Sponsor calls; Meet with logistic teams; Solicit goody bag donations*	*Close out sponsors; Order benefit items; Recruit players*

Staying the Course: An Implementation Process

* Development Committee meets six times throughout the year to review plan progress and, with Development Director, will identify problems and solutions.

* Development Director and Committee Chair discuss development issues on a regular basis.

* Committee Chair and Development Director monitor sub-committee chairs; Committee Chair follows up on any problems.

* Development Committee discusses fund development plan and progress at monthly board meetings.

* Development Director provides financial and statistical data with which to help evaluate progress of the plan.

   WEEKLY
   * Development Director reviews high-level strategy (plan) and fund reports compared against goals and previous year (donor database or accounting software).
   * Responsible party for each goal conducts weekly report of measurement and reports to Development Director and/or board and Committee Chairs as appropriate.

   MONTHLY
   * Development Director updates each measurable goal and reports to accountable parties

   QUARTERLY
   * Board reports year-to-date; year against goals; year over previous year

   ANNUAL
   * Numerical and narrative report to board and donors establishing progress against plan/proposal

A Few Parting Words from Our Expert...

Yes, it is a lot of work putting your plan together. No, everything will not work out. Sometimes, even better opportunities will lead you to drop one method for another. However, having a plan, as flawed by the unknown as it may be, will give your organization the highest probability of fundraising success and organizational cohesiveness as a bonus.

All of the plans in the world are only as good as the impact of your work on people's lives. When people choose to give a gift, they are impacted. How much depends on your relationship with them. How and how often you thank them and share the narrative stories and the strategic "measurables" of how their dollar made your work possible, is directly related to the donor's tendency to give again.

Never forget to say "thank you" more than you say "please give."

Results and appreciation: the best tonic for donor fatigue.

Part 6
Communication: Telling Your Story

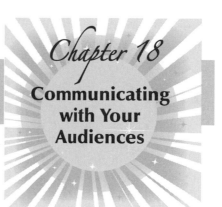

Chapter 18

Communicating with Your Audiences

"It is from the numberless diverse acts of courage and belief that human history is shaped. Each time a man stands up for an ideal or acts to improve the lot of others or strikes out against injustice, he sends forth a tiny ripple of hope, and crossing each other from a million different centers of energy and daring, those ripples build a current that can sweep down the mightiest walls of oppression and resistance."

~Robert F. Kennedy

As an up-and-coming nonprofit organization, you and your team will need to communicate with a wide variety of audiences. Each group will have different needs and preferred methods of communication. You will need to cater your message to reach your donors, prospects, program participants, board members, staff, volunteers, members, and the community-at-large.

Before launching a communications plan, you should have specific outcomes that you expect. The outcomes should be precise and measurable. For example, if you are attempting to recruit new volunteers with a communications piece, you should see a spike in the size of your volunteer corps, as well as the number of volunteer hours. (Remember to track the number of volunteers and volunteer hours for your annual audit report. Many donor databases have the capability to track this information. In the beginning, you can create an Excel spreadsheet.)

Here are some audience groups along with the major types of mediums you may be interested in creating.

Donors

Never underestimate the importance of continued and effective communication with your donors. It will require some testing and adjusting to find the right mix of messages and mediums your organization will need to utilize to reach your diverse donor base. Two of the most common methods are direct mail and newsletters.

Direct Mail

Direct mail remains a low-cost option to reach the majority of your audience. For direct mail to be successful, you must ensure that your development team keeps an accurate donor database with current contact information for your constituents. You should ask for contact information from your supporters at every event. Be creative—have a drawing and ask for contact information—include a statement that by entering the drawing, the person is giving permission to be contacted via email or postal mail.

It is difficult to find the right balance between informing your audience and asking for support. If you contact your donors too often, they may feel your organization is invasive. I would recommend that you not make contact with your donors more often than quarterly.

Newsletters

Using newsletters to share your organization's good work is an excellent way to reach your audience. You can choose to print your newsletter, as well as provide an electronic version via email. The purpose of the newsletter is to show your supporters what goals have been achieved and what is planned in the next few months. Make sure you use this opportunity to ask for financial support. You may want to include a "wish list" of items that your organization is hoping to receive in-kind.

Prospects

Your organization will want to continually cultivate new donors and members. The best way to provide an overview of your organization and its programs and services is to prepare a marketing or solicitation package. You will include membership brochures, your most recent annual report (if available), copies of any media write-ups, invitations, and any other printed materials. It is a good idea to have several packages prepared at all times. That way if you have unexpected guests, you can quickly pull these packages for the group.

You and your development team should have a top-50 list of prospects. The list should be organized by the likelihood of turning the prospect into a donor. So, number one on the list should be the donor (individual or couple, corporation or foundation) that is most likely to give first. The list should provide details of the donor's previous giving or involvement with your organization; the staff member, volunteer, or board member that has a relationship or connection to the donor; contact schedule; and any other pertinent information, like their known giving history (the donor supports children's educational programming, general, arts & culture, etc.). This list should be continually evaluated and updated. I recommend that this list remain confidential.

Members

Depending on the type of organization you create, your member base will be an extremely important and valuable group. Unrestricted revenues are hard to come by and the fees generated by memberships can provide a level of predictable income year after year.

Cultivation and retention will be the primary solicitation reasons you will communicate with your members. This group should be on your newsletter list and may receive invitations to "member-only" events and programs. Make sure that this group is treated as VIPs.

Program Participants

If your organization will provide public programming, you will create a mailing list (print or electronic) of people that have expressed an interest or have attended a previous program. You can also add the members of any special interest groups. For example, if you are opening an art museum and are planning a photography exhibit, you will want to contact photography groups and the photography department at your local colleges.

In addition, you will be relying on your program participants to complete surveys to aid in the improvement of your educational offerings. You may want to provide a reward of some type to ensure a higher response rate. A free membership, tickets to an upcoming program, lunch or dinner (perhaps you can get the restaurant to donate the meal!), or a logo item advertising your agency all make for a nice thank-you gift.

In addition to the external groups we have already explored, you will be communicating with a variety of internal groups, as well. Here is an overview of the primary groups and the motivations for communicating with them.

Board Members

In Part 2, we talked about building a successful board of directors. Your first interaction with a potential board member will likely include a prospect package to provide the person with an excellent introduction to your organization. Hopefully, your first meeting will prove fruitful and the person will agree to join the board.

After their nomination is approved by the board, your new board member will attend an orientation session, where you will provide the director with the well-designed board manual. Take your time in planning the contents of the board manual and make sure that it provides an appropriate overview of the organization's expectations, organizational history, structure, and future strategic plans.

Your board members should be on most every mailing list for your organization. This group is internal, but also remains an external part of your organization. It will send a strong message to the community if the majority of your board members attend your programs and events to show their support. Likewise, if a large percentage of your board members fail to attend your events, it tells the community that the directors do not support your mission. The community will question why they should offer support if the board members don't.

Board members will likely be a group of high-level executives and business or community leaders. You will have to be a strong leader to manage this group of volunteers. This group will come from varying backgrounds and will approach business decisions from different perspectives. You and your board chair will have to work overtime to keep the group on task and working toward the organization's strategic goals. To keep the directors energized and focused, you will want to provide regular updates between board meetings. This can be achieved via an email to the group with organizational highlights.

For each scheduled board meeting, you and your team will prepare a packet of materials that must be professional in appearance, with accurate and concise content. The packet should be rather standard—an agenda, the prior meeting's minutes for review and approval, the CEO's report, the financials, the development report, a calendar, and overview of upcoming events. It will be helpful to keep the same standard and predictable information for presentation during the meeting.

Proper governance relies on the continual appraisal of the board's performance and their impressions of the organization's work toward strategic goal attainment. Work closely with your board chair or an outside consultant to design surveys to aid the board in their appraisal process. Because of their dual role as internal and external constituents, their impressions will be unique and very helpful in evaluating your organization's goals.

Staff

Your staff is the organization's public "face." Many of your audience members will interact with your staff more than with you and your board of directors. As your organization's front line, you will want to provide training, mentoring, and continual updates. The best way to reach your staff as a whole is to have regular staff meetings. I like to have a weekly staff meeting with each member updating the group on the current status of their individual/departmental projects and what is on the horizon in their departments.

As in any organization, your staff is your most valuable asset. It would be impossible for you to fulfill your mission without their talent, expertise, and dedication. Never forget to show your appreciation for their hard work. The staff meeting is another platform for you to provide public recognition for staff members' accomplishments. The staff meeting should be used as a pep rally of sorts. I prefer to keep the energy positive and forward-looking and not to allow the group to get bogged down in finger pointing and negativity.

Volunteers

Your agency will be communicating with your current volunteer corps, as well as participating in communication tactics to attract new volunteers. You will want to ensure that you have an excellent volunteer database to help manage this important group. You should add your volunteers to your member mailing list and/or newsletter list. They, too, will serve as the organization's front line. This group will demand current and relevant information about what is going on within the organization.

Recruitment of volunteers is an art form. You can rely on word of mouth from your current volunteers and augment this effort with volunteer events and special access to organizational programs and events. Your volunteers will be a demographically diverse group, so be creative in designing programs that will appeal to different types of people.

Community

Every form of communication has the potential to reach the community-at-large, so you should keep this in mind when creating any marketing materials. Your ultimate goal should be to reach as many people as possible, to recruit as many volunteers and supporters as possible and to improve the lives of the people you will serve. With any new business, there will be a continual trial-and-error approach. Something I've learned working in the nonprofit world is that you will get a lot of advice from others. As difficult as it may be, listen intently to this "free" advice and decide if it applies to your organization or not. Occasionally, the advice will yield a wonderful nugget of genius and provide the impetus to propel your organization to the next level.

Chapter 19

Delivering the Message

"Life's most persistent and urgent question is,
What are you doing for others?"

~Martin Luther King, Jr.

In Chapter 18, we discussed the various audiences that you will need to reach through your marketing and public relations efforts. Now let's touch on the assorted avenues you can use to share your story. You will want to research the methods that are working for your community partners and if possible, to what level of success. It will save you some time and money to learn what local donors are expecting and accustomed to receiving from other nonprofits.

Public Relations

The events and programs planned and executed by your organization should capture the interest of the community and with any luck, the interest of the media. Try to capitalize on any national or international events that coincide with your mission. For example, if your organization provides services for clients with HIV/AIDS, you will want to grab the local media's attention on World AIDS Day. Your organization could host a symposium featuring renowned educators and medical professionals providing the latest information on current studies.

Your marketing team can alert the media to newsworthy events by sending press releases to the newswire. Your organization will likely incur an expense, but the attention could provide an excellent return on your investment. There are multiple samples of press releases available on the Internet. Make sure you present your organization in a professional manner.

Direct Mail

Direct mail is still a lower cost option to reach your entire audience. For direct mail to be successful, you must ensure that you keep an accurate donor database with current contact information for your constituents. You should ask for contact information from your supporters at every event. Be creative—have a drawing and ask for contact information—include a statement that by entering the drawing, the person is giving permission to be contacted via email or postal mail.

It is difficult to find the right mix of informing your audience and asking for support. If you contact your donors too often, they may feel your organization is invasive. I would recommend that you not contact your donors more than quarterly.

Newsletters

Using newsletters to share your organization's good work is an excellent way to reach your audience. You can choose to print your newsletter, as well as provide an electronic version via email. The purpose of the newsletter is to show your supporters what goals have been achieved and what is planned in the next few months. Make sure you use this opportunity to ask for financial support. You may want to include a "wish list" of items that your organization is hoping to receive in-kind.

Social Media

Social media is a gift to nonprofit organizations because of the minimal financial costs. You may choose to share photos from your programs and events on Flickr, design and manage an organizational Facebook page, provide interesting information on Twitter, upload videos to YouTube, and without a doubt, you will want a thorough organizational website.

My dear friend and social media queen, Eve Mayer Orsburn, provides the following case study from her must-have book, *Social Media for the CEO*.

Case Study: *Mayo Clinic*

Organization: Mayo Clinic (http://www.mayoclinic.org)

Background: Mayo Clinic is a not-for-profit medical practice dedicated to the diagnosis and treatment of virtually every type of complex illness.

Business Need: To leverage Mayo Clinic's established reputation in direct promotion rather than relying only on third-party media representation. In short, "Don't just pitch the media, be the media."

Social Media Solution: A custom YouTube channel to serve as a platform to distribute syndicated press-package videos created for traditional TV news and information to the media parties interested in featuring Mayo Clinic.

Business Result: Very large numbers of viewers (currently more than 3,000,000) means a lot of exposure. Thanks to low production costs on many of the clips, any return on investment is significant. This channel has become a destination within itself and a way for Mayo Clinic to leverage its reputation without having to always use a third party. Furthermore, the YouTube channel has become a place for amateur and casual videos.

What Actually Happened: Lee Aase, Manager, Syndication and Social Media, at Mayo Clinic notes that for more than 100 years, Mayo Clinic has relied almost completely on word of mouth and third-party media to spread its reputation. Because social media is the new word of mouth, the various platforms available fit in perfectly with the clinic's traditional means of promotion. Plus, it affords Mayo Clinic the opportunity to use its own reputation to its advantage.

(continued)

As Mr. Aase has stated, "Don't just pitch the media, be the media," meaning Mayo Clinic has a very strong reputation and does not have to rely solely on third-party media representation to establish credibility. They already have a lot of credibility in their field, and can use that as a way to appeal to a wider audience.

In addition, because the clinic is a not-for-profit organization, there is less pressure to see an immediate return on investment and more opportunity to use social media in a purely altruistic sense. Of course, this also brings greater social media success, because social media is often about sharing valuable information.

The implementation of a YouTube channel provides the clinic with another platform to utilize the 90-second to two-minute syndicated press-package videos created for traditional TV news and information to the media parties interested in featuring Mayo Clinic. It also creates a platform to pitch to traditional media, as well as reinforces the clinic's established reputation by providing information and advice to patient communities, speeding up the dissemination of medical information on rare or specialized illnesses to people across the world at a rate never experienced before. Although there is not as strong a focus on ROI as there might be in a corporation, Mr. Aase explains that the clinic still sees new patients coming in because of content they viewed on Mayo Clinic's YouTube channel.

A perfect example is the $10^1/_2$-minute video of Mayo Clinic's Dr. Mesa discussing myelofibrosis, a rare form of blood cancer, which was shot with a simple $150 Flip camera. This video has been viewed more than 6,000 times, and more than 50 out-of-state patients who chose Mayo Clinic because they saw this video have contacted Dr. Mesa. Not only does this video provide necessary information to potential patients, the clinic's ROI from making that information widely available through YouTube is substantial.

One key element in the clinic's social media strategy is the interconnectedness across platforms. Mayo Clinic maintains a Twitter feed, a Facebook page, a YouTube channel, and several blogs. Mr. Aase says these different channels are all crucial to a successful social media campaign.

(continued)

In July 2010, Mayo Clinic increased its commitment to using social media by creating Mayo Clinic Center for Social Media. The center's purpose is to go beyond the public relations and marketing uses of social media, and to use variations of these tools throughout the organization. Through the center, Mayo aims to accelerate adoption of social media in clinical practice, education, research, and administration.

The center's focus is not only internal to Mayo Clinic, however. The center also will be a resource for other hospitals and health-related organizations looking for guidance in applying social media. "Many staff in healthcare organizations who are interested in using social media have pointed to our Mayo Clinic example to help make their case to leadership," Mr. Aase explains. "Through the center, we have a way for them to join a formal network, and to get access to materials and resources to support their venture into social media."

Mr. Aase says the network will not be limited to medical providers. It will also include nonprofit health-related organizations and associations. "We want to be a resource to any organization looking for ways to apply social media to improve health," he says. "Our fundamental goal is to help patients through social media, whether that means giving them increased access to scientific information or helping them to get together and learn from each other, becoming active partners with their healthcare providers. We also want to help medical professionals in research and education connect with each other, and are eager to play a role in spreading the use of these powerful communication tools throughout the health system."

For more information about Mayo Clinic Center for Social Media, visit http://socialmedia.mayoclinic.org.

As the case study indicates, social media can provide a terrific return on what is usually a small investment, comparatively speaking. Explore the options and pick what makes the most sense for your organization. Always start with something that will be manageable; you don't want your organization's online image to be stale or out-dated.

Annual Report

Although not legally required, most nonprofit organizations produce an annual report that is mailed to current and potential donors. The annual report is another opportunity to share your organization's successes—programmatically, financially, and otherwise. This report should be specific about your accomplishments and clearly demonstrate the good work your organization is doing in the community. If you have reached a milestone, play it up big! If you've built a new building, use that as your theme, especially if you have major donors whose names will appear on the structure. If your organization provides direct services, include a client's story in your annual report. You may want to include a profile of a volunteer, a staff member, and a board member.

Another important purpose of your annual report will be properly thanking all of the supporters that made your achievements possible. Many nonprofits list the donors at the end of the report alphabetically in giving level categories. You can choose whatever format works for you and your organization.

The financial section should be easy to read. Many nonprofits present their financial results in pie charts or bar graphs. The overview should indicate the total amount and types of support and how the organization spent the dollars. Depending on the timing of the report and your annual audit, the numbers may be audited or unaudited. Make sure that you state whether the results are audited or not.

Grant Reports

Many foundations and government funders will require interim and final grant reports. Don't forget to start with the original proposal to ensure you respond to the goals and purposes you laid out originally. It will be in your best interest (and easiest!) to focus on the same message in all of your communications. Have your running list of accomplishments and tell the story every chance you get. You can control your message and give your supporters the information they need to advocate for your cause.

Notes, Cards, and Letters

Your relationship and amount of contact with constituents will dictate the type of communication you send. I try to send personal notes as often as possible. Personally, if I receive a handwritten note, I will read the message in its entirety. I may be old-school, but it does make me feel special to know that someone has taken the time to write a personal note. A colleague of mine has a goal to send at least one thank-you card each day. Although I plan to send more notes, this task always ends up on my New Year's resolution list.

If your time will not allow for handwritten notes, send typewritten thank-you letters. Bottom line—thank your donors in a timely manner in the most appropriate means possible.

Personal vs. Public Recognition

You really have to listen to your donors and learn if they prefer personal or public recognition. If a donor supports your capital campaign via a naming opportunity, it should be clear that they are comfortable with public recognition. Other philanthropists prefer to quietly support causes that are near and dear to their hearts. Make sure you do your homework and learn about your donors' personalities. Not thanking a donor in the appropriate manner jeopardizes future support. Once you and your team have done the background work and learned your donors' preferences, make sure you enter the information into the notes section of your donor database.

Chapter 20

Agility: Making Adjustments

"The measure of a life is not its duration, but its donation."
~Peter Marshall

In today's economy, one of the secrets to success is to remain agile and continually review your mission and how your organization is working toward achieving its strategic goals. Frequently, nonprofit organizations will find funding for a specific purpose and then design a new program to satisfy the funding requirements. You may find that these knee-jerk decisions are not closely aligned with your mission. As Tina McIntosh shared with us, she and the staff of Joy's House get together annually and review all of their programs and services to ensure that they are remaining true to their mission. This process allows Joy's House to remain an efficient and focused organization and their guests are the real winners by receiving the services they need most.

I realize now that we are nearing the end of this guide and I haven't properly introduced you to the organization that my husband and I started together, Texas Junior Anglers. The organization is the result of my husband making an adjustment in his career—remaining agile and overcoming obstacles during a professionally challenging period in his life.

Case Study

Name of nonprofit organization: Texas Junior Anglers, Inc.

Address: Arlington, Texas

Telephone: (817) 516-0532

Website: www.texasjunioranglers.org

Date of incorporation: 2001

Founder(s): Jeff Scott, President

Inspiration: Jeff, a native Texan, spends much of his free time enjoying a variety of outdoor activities. He worked for a similar organization for several years, and when his contract was not renewed, he set about starting TJA. Jeff is hopeful that through his work in the community, his organization can increase community park attendance, educate young people about the environment, and spark a passion for the outdoors in future generations.

Background/community need: Over the past couple of decades, family activities have changed dramatically with more people spending their free time indoors. TJA and similar outreach organizations hope to generate interest in our natural resources, conservation, and the outdoor sports opportunities offered at community parks. Fishing, in particular, is an equal opportunity sport. With reasonable accommodations, most individuals are able to actively participate.

(continued)

Organization's mission: Texas Junior Anglers is an outreach program designed to provide educational opportunities for children (ages 16 and under) regarding aquatic stewardship and conservation of our natural resources, fostering strong familial relationships within targeted communities, and enabling all children to participate in outdoor recreation.

Organization's vision: TJA strives to increase park attendance by instilling a passion for the state's natural resources and recreational opportunities.

Were the required filings completed internally or by an external expert? Jeff and I were able to complete initial filings on our own. We asked our friends for advice and guidance, and used the resources available in our local library, online sources, as well as printed publications.

Organizational challenges/solutions: The biggest challenge for Jeff and TJA is the staff size; Jeff is the only paid employee. During the busy spring and summer seasons, Jeff augments his staff with contract employees. It is always a struggle for Jeff to balance the back office priorities with the execution of the program. It remains a goal to increase the annual budget through additional funding sources, paving the way to build the organizational capacity.

Organizational successes: Since inception, TJA has held thousands of events and reached tens of thousands of children and adults. Through the recession, Jeff has been able to attract new events and will continue to educate young people about the importance of conserving our natural resources and spread the joy of outdoor recreational opportunities to future generations.

As this final chapter comes to a close, I hope that you have gained the courage and knowledge necessary for you to take the steps toward starting your new nonprofit organization. Working in the nonprofit field has provided numerous rewards for me. I wish you the best in your journey and I look forward to applauding your achievements and living in a world in which all are given the opportunity to thrive.

Appendix

Filing Information

The information on the following pages is provided to offer you general information and save you some valuable time in your research, but by no means is all-inclusive. Some states have made the process of starting a nonprofit much easier than others. The information on the following pages is for domestic nonprofit organizations.

Here is a quick checklist to help guide you through this process:

* Draft organization's bylaws
* Select (if you haven't done so by now) your board of directors
* Prepare a budget and anticipated financial statements for the next three years
* Hold a board meeting and elect officers
* Draft Articles of Incorporation and file with your state
* Reserve/register your organization's name
* File and obtain your organization's Employer Identification Number (EIN) using IRS Form SS-4

The form can be filed online or by mail, phone, or fax:

> EIN Operations
> Cincinnati, OH 45999
> Telephone: 800-829-4933
> FAX: 859-669-5760
> Web: http://www.irs.gov/pub/irs-pdf/fss4.pdf

* Complete and file IRS Form 1023 (with appropriate fee—either $400 or $850) to obtain federal designation as a 501(c)(3) charitable, exempt organization and mail to:

  > Internal Revenue Service
  > Post Office Box 12192
  > Covington, KY 41012-0192
  > Web: http://www.irs.gov/pub/irs-pdf/f1023.pdf

* File the registration documents with your state to solicit charitable donations

* File annual reports with the Secretary of State in the state in which your organization is registered, if required

* File annual renewals as a registered organization able to solicit charitable donations in your state, if required

* File annual reports (Form 990 or 990-EZ) with the Internal Revenue Service

* File payroll reports and pay payroll taxes to the appropriate agencies

The bylaws will serve as your organization's official operating policies and procedures manual. Bylaws must clearly define:

* Size of the board and how it will function

* Roles and duties of directors and officers

* Rules and procedures for holding meetings, electing directors, and appointing officers

* Other essential corporate governance matters, including the role of board committees

Your state's laws governing charitable organizations typically address non-profit governance matters. Of course, you may choose different rules, as long as they aren't in violation of state law and are specifically included in your bylaws. If you choose to follow state law, restating them in your bylaws ensures that all your operating rules are in one document.

Your organization's bylaws are not public documents, but you should consider making them readily available to provide transparency and encourage your board of directors to pay close attention to them. Your bylaws should be reviewed regularly by the board of directors and amended as the organization grows and evolves.

If your state requires exempt organizations to file annual returns, you must report name, address, and structural and operational changes to your bylaws on the return. Some states may also require you to file bylaws and report changes.

Please be aware that bylaws are very specific for each organization, so you will want to change them to meet your nonprofit organization's needs.

For your convenience, a sample copy of bylaws is provided below:

BYLAWS OF
OF

_____

A Nonprofit Corporation

ARTICLE I — OFFICES

Section 1 — Name: The principal office of the Corporation shall be located in the City of _____, County of _____, within the State of _____. The Corporation may also maintain offices at such other places as the board of directors may, from time to time, determine.

ARTICLE II — PURPOSE

Section 1 — Internal Revenue Code, Section 501(c)(3) Purpose: Said Corporation is organized exclusively for charitable, religious, educational, or scientific purposes, including for such purposed, the making of distributions to organizations that qualify as exempt organizations under section 501(c)(3) of the Internal Revenue Code, or the corresponding section of any future tax code. The specific purpose of the Corporation is:

_____

_____

_____

_____

_____

_____.

Section 2 — No private inurement: No part of the net earnings of the corporation shall inure to the benefit of or be distributable to its members, trustees, officers, or other private persons, except that of the Corporation shall be authorized and empowered to pay reasonable compensation for services rendered and to make payments and distributions in furtherance of the purposes set forth in Section 1 hereof.

(continued)

BYLAWS (continued)

Section 3 — No lobbying activities: No substantial part of the activities of the Corporation shall be the carrying on of propaganda, or otherwise attempting to influence legislation, and the Corporation shall not participate in, or intervene in any political campaign on behalf of or in opposition to any candidate for public office. Notwithstanding any other provision of these articles, this Corporation shall not engage in any activities or exercise any powers that are not in furtherance of the purposes of the Corporation.

ARTICLE III — DIRECTORS

Section 1 — Number: The number of initial directors (members) of this corporation shall be _____ and collectively, they will be known as the board of directors. This number can be increased/decreased by the amendment of these bylaws by the board, but shall in no case be fewer than _____ director(s).

Section 2 — Duties: It shall be the duty of the Corporation's directors to:

- Perform any and all duties imposed on them either collectively or individually by law, by the Articles of Incorporation, or by these bylaws;
- Appoint and remove, employ and discharge, and except as otherwise provided in these bylaws, prescribe the duties and determine the compensation of all officers, agents, and employees of the corporation;
- Supervise all officers, agents, and employees of the corporation to ensure that their duties are performed satisfactorily and efficiently;
- Meet at such times and places as required by these bylaws; and
- Register their addresses with the Secretary of the board of the corporation and notices of meetings delivered to them at such address shall be valid.

Section 3 — Terms: Board members shall serve ____-year terms, but are eligible for re-election for up to _____ consecutive terms.

(continued)

BYLAWS (continued)

Section 4 — Resignation, termination, and absences: Any officer may resign at any time by providing written notice to the Corporation's board Chair and/or board Secretary. Such resignation shall take effect immediately upon certification of the Secretary. Board members may be terminated from the board due to excessive absences, without prior approval. A board member may be removed, with or without cause, by a majority vote of the remaining directors.

Section 5 — Vacancies: When a vacancy on the board arises, the Secretary or Chair of the nominating committee must receive nominations for new members from present board members in advance of a scheduled board meeting. The nominations, along with the nominees' resumes, shall be sent out to board members with the regular board meeting announcement, to be voted upon at the next board meeting.

Section 6 — Meetings and notice: The board shall meet _____ (times per year), at an agreed-upon time and place. An official board meeting requires that each board member have written notice in advance.

Section 7 — Special meetings: Special meetings of the board shall be called upon the request of the Chair, or one-third of the board. Notices of special meetings shall be sent out by the Secretary to each board member at least two weeks in advance.

Section 8 — Quorum for meetings: A quorum for the Corporation's board of directors shall require _____% of the members of the board of directors.

Except as otherwise provided under the Articles of Incorporation, these Bylaws, or provision of law, no business shall be considered by the board at any meeting at which the required quorum is not present and the only motion the chair shall entertain is the motion to adjourn.

Section 9 — Election procedures: New directors shall be elected by a majority of directors present at such a meeting, provided there is a quorum present. Directors so elected shall serve a term beginning

_____.

(continued)

BYLAWS (continued)

Section 10 — Officers and duties: There shall be a minimum of four officers of the board, consisting of a Chair, Vice-Chair, Secretary, and Treasurer. Their duties are as follows:

> The *Chair* shall convene regularly scheduled board meetings, shall preside or arrange for other members of the Executive Committee to preside at each meeting in the following order: Vice-chair, Secretary, and then Treasurer.

> The *Vice-Chair* shall chair committees on special subjects as designated by the board.

> The *Secretary* shall be responsible for keeping records of board actions, including overseeing the taking of minutes at all board meetings, sending out meeting announcements, distributing copies of minutes and the agenda to each board member, and assuring that corporate records are properly maintained.

> The *Treasurer* shall make a report at each board meeting. The Treasurer shall chair the finance committee and ensure accurate financial information is available to board members and the public.

ARTICLE IV — COMMITTEES

Section 1 — Committee formation: The board may create committees as needed, such as fundraising, programming, public relations/marketing, audit, etc. The board Chair appoints all Committee Chairs.

Section 2 — Executive Committee: The four officers serve as the members of the Executive Committee. Except for the power to amend the Articles of Incorporation and bylaws, the Executive Committee shall have all the powers and authority of the board of directors in the intervals between meetings of the board of directors, and is subject to the direction and control of the full board.

(continued)

BYLAWS (continued)

Section 3 — Finance Committee: The Treasurer is the chair of the Finance Committee, which should include at least three other independent members. The Finance Committee is responsible for developing and reviewing fiscal procedures and the annual budget with staff and other board members. The board must approve the budget and all expenditures must be within budget. Any major change in the budget must be approved by the board or the Executive Committee. The fiscal year shall be _____. Annual reports are required to be submitted to the board showing income, expenditures, and pending income. The financial records of the organization are public information and shall be made available to the members, board members, and the public-at-large.

ARTICLE V — AMENDMENTS

Section 1 — Amendments: These bylaws may be amended when necessary by a majority vote of the board of directors. Proposed amendments must be submitted to the Secretary and included with regular board announcements.

ARTICLE VI — INDEMNIFICATION

Section 1 — Indemnification: Any officer, director, or employee of the Corporation shall be indemnified and held harmless to the full extent allowed by law.

Section 2 — Insurance: The Corporation shall obtain insurance providing for indemnification of directors, officers, and employees.

The bylaws of the Corporation have been adopted and certified by the board of directors on _____.

Secretary_____

Date _____

Articles of Incorporation

As you work through your research, you may find that your state's sample Articles of Incorporation do not meet IRS standards. It is in your best interest to draft one set of articles satisfying both state and federal guidelines.

IRS Required Language for Nonprofit Articles of Incorporation

Said organization is organized exclusively for charitable, religious, educational, and scientific purposes, including, for such purposes, the making of distributions to organizations that qualify as exempt organizations under section 501 (c) (3) of the Internal Revenue Code, or corresponding section of any future federal tax code.

No part of the net earnings of the organization shall inure to the benefit of, or be distributable to its members, trustees, officers, or other private persons, except that the organization shall be authorized and empowered to pay reasonable compensation for services rendered and to make payments and distributions in furtherance of the purposes set forth in the purpose clause hereof. No substantial part of the activities of the organization shall be the carrying on of propaganda, or otherwise attempting to influence legislation, and the organization shall not participate in, or intervene in (including the publishing or distribution of statements) any political campaign on behalf of any candidate for public office. Notwithstanding any other provision of this document, the organization shall not carry on any other activities not permitted to be carried on (a) by any organization exempt from federal income tax under section 501 (c) (3) of the Internal Revenue Code, corresponding section of any future federal tax code, or (b) by an organization, contributions to which are deductible under section 170 (c) (2) of the Internal Revenue Code, or corresponding section of any future federal tax code.

Upon the dissolution of the organization, assets shall be distributed for one or more exempt purposes within the meaning of section 501 (c) (3) of the Internal Revenue Code, or corresponding section of any future federal tax code, or shall be distributed to the federal government, or to a state or local government, for the public purpose. Any such assets not disposed of shall be disposed of by the Court of Common Pleas of the county in which the principle office of the organization is then located, exclusively for the purposes or to such organization or organizations, as said court shall determine, which are organized and operated exclusively for such purposes.

ARTICLES OF INCORPORATION
OF

A Nonprofit Corporation

Pursuant to the provision of the Nonprofit Corporation Act of this state, the undersigned incorporator(s) adopt the following Articles of Incorporation to form a nonprofit corporation.

ARTICLE I — NAME, PURPOSE, AND DURATION

Section 1 — Name: The name of the organization shall be _____. It shall be a nonprofit organization incorporated under the laws of the state of _____.

The name and address of the registered agent and registered offices of this corporation are:

_____
_____
_____
_____
_____.

Section 2 — Purpose: The purposes for which **[Insert name of nonprofit]** is organized are for the following charitable, scientific, or educational purposes:

_____
_____
_____
_____
_____.

Section 3 — Duration: The period of the duration of this corporation is:
_____.

(continued)

ARTICLES OF INCORPORATION (continued)

Section 4 — Dissolution: Upon the dissolution of the corporation, assets shall be distributed for one or more exempt purposes within the meaning of section 501(c)(3) of the Internal Revenue Code, or the corresponding section of any future federal tax code, or shall be distributed to the federal government, or to a state or local government, for a public purpose. Any such assets not so disposed shall be disposed of by a Court of Competent Jurisdiction of the county in which the principal office of the corporation is then located, exclusively for such purposes or to such organizations, as said Court shall determine, which are operated exclusively for such purposes.

ARTICLE II — BOARD OF DIRECTORS

Section 1 — Membership: The number of initial directors (members) of this corporation shall be _____ and their names and addresses are:

_____

_____

_____

_____.

Section 2 — Board role and size: The board is responsible for overall policy and direction of the organization, and formally entrusts the responsibility of day-to-day operations to the Executive Director and staff.

Section 3 — Compensation: No part of the net earnings of the corporation shall inure to the benefit of or be distributable to its members, trustees, officers, or other private persons, except that of the corporation shall be authorized and empowered to pay reasonable compensation for services rendered and to make payments and distributions in furtherance of the purposes set forth in Article I, Section 2 hereof. No substantial part of the activities of the corporation shall be the carrying on of propaganda, or otherwise attempting to influence legislation, and the corporation shall not participate in, or intervene in any political campaign on behalf of or in opposition to any candidate for public office. Notwithstanding any other provision of these articles, this corporation shall not except to an

(continued)

ARTICLES OF INCORPORATION (continued)

insubstantial degree, engage in any activities or exercise any powers that are not in furtherance of the purposes of the corporation. In as such, board members will serve as volunteers, without compensation other than the reimbursement of reasonable expenses related to their service to the organization.

Section 4 — Terms: All board members shall serve ____-year terms, but are eligible for re-election for up to _____ consecutive terms.

Section 5 — Meetings and notice: The board shall meet _____, at an agreed-upon time and place. An official board meeting requires that each board member have written notice at least two weeks in advance.

Section 6 — Board elections: During the last meeting of each fiscal year of the corporation, the board of directors shall elect directors to replace those whose terms will expire at the end of the fiscal year. This election shall take place during a regular meeting of the directors, called in accordance with the provisions of these bylaws.

Section 7 — Election procedures: New directors shall be elected by a majority of directors present at such a meeting, provided there is a quorum present. Directors so elected shall serve a term beginning _____.

Section 8 — Quorum: A quorum must be attended by at least _____ percent of board members for business transactions to take place and motions to pass.

Section 9 — Officers and duties: There shall be a minimum of four officers of the board, consisting of a Chair, Vice-chair, Secretary, and Treasurer. Their duties are as follows:

> The *Chair* shall convene regularly scheduled board meetings, shall preside or arrange for other members of the Executive Committee to preside at each meeting in the following order: Vice-chair, Secretary, and then Treasurer.

(continued)

ARTICLES OF INCORPORATION (continued)

The *Vice-chair* shall chair committees on special subjects as designated by the board.

The *Secretary* shall be responsible for keeping records of board actions, including overseeing the taking of minutes at all board meetings, sending out meeting announcements, distributing copies of minutes and the agenda to each board member, and assuring that corporate records are maintained.

The *Treasurer* shall make a report at each board meeting. The Treasurer shall chair the finance committee and ensure accurate financial information is available to board members and the public.

Section 10 — Vacancies: When a vacancy on the board arises, the Secretary or Chair of the nominating committee must receive nominations for new members from present board members in advance of a scheduled board meeting. The nominations, along with the nominees' resumes, shall be sent out to board members with the regular board meeting announcement, to be voted upon at the next board meeting.

Section 11 — Resignation, termination, and absences: Resignation from the board should be in writing and certified by the Secretary. Board members may be terminated from the board due to excessive absences, without prior approval. A board member may be removed for other reasons by a majority vote of the remaining directors.

Section 12 — Special meetings: Special meetings of the board shall be called upon the request of the Chair, or one-third of the board. Notices of special meetings shall be sent out by the Secretary to each board member at least two weeks in advance.

ARTICLE III — COMMITTEES

Section 1 — Committee formation: The board may create committees as needed, such as fundraising, programming, public relations/marketing, audit, etc. The board Chair appoints all Committee Chairs.

(continued)

ARTICLES OF INCORPORATION (continued)

Section 2 — Executive Committee: The four officers serve as the members of the Executive Committee. Except for the power to amend the Articles of Incorporation and bylaws, the Executive Committee shall have all the powers and authority of the board of directors in the intervals between meetings of the board of directors, and is subject to the direction and control of the full board.

Section 3 — Finance Committee: The Treasurer is the chair of the Finance Committee, which includes three other board members. The Finance Committee is responsible for developing and reviewing fiscal procedures and the annual budget with staff and other board members. The board must approve the budget and all expenditures must be within budget. Any major change in the budget must be approved by the board or the Executive Committee. The fiscal year shall be _____. Annual reports are required to be submitted to the board showing income, expenditures, and pending income. The financial records of the organization are public information and shall be made available to the members, board members, as well as the public-at-large.

ARTICLE IV — EXECUTIVE DIRECTOR AND STAFF

Section 1 — Executive Director: The Executive Director is selected and hired by the board. The Executive Director has day-to-day responsibilities for the organization, including the fulfillment of the organization's strategic plan. The Executive Director will attend all board meetings, reporting on the progress of the organization. The board may designate other duties as necessary.

ARTICLE V — AMENDMENTS

Section 1 — Amendments: These bylaws may be amended when necessary by a majority vote of the board of directors. Proposed amendments must be submitted to the Secretary and included with regular board announcements.

(continued)

ARTICLES OF INCORPORATION (continued)

CERTIFICATION

These undersigned incorporator(s) hereby declare under penalty of perjury that the statements made in the foregoing Articles of Incorporation are true. Furthermore, these bylaws were approved by the board of directors on _____.

Incorporator_____

Date _____

Incorporator_____

Date _____

Incorporator_____

Date _____

Incorporator_____

Date _____

Incorporator_____

Date _____

IRS Form SS-4: Application for Employer Identification Number

Note: The Instructions for Form SS-4 begin on the next page of this document.

Attention

Limit of five (5) Employer Identification Number (EIN) Assignments per Business Day

Due to a high volume of requests for EINs, the IRS will begin limiting the number

of EINs assigned per day to a responsible party identified on Form SS-4.

Effective April 11, 2011, a responsible party will be limited to **five (5) EINs** in one

business day. This limit is in effect whether you apply online, by phone, fax, or

mail.

Instructions for Form SS-4

Department of the Treasury
Internal Revenue Service

(Rev. January 2011)

Application for Employer Identification Number (EIN)
Use with the January 2010 revision of Form SS-4

Section references are to the Internal Revenue Code unless otherwise noted.

What's New

EIN operations contact information. Contact information for EIN operations at the Philadelphia Internal Revenue Service Center has changed.
• The phone number to use for Form SS-4 applicants outside of the United States has changed to 1-267-941-1099. See the *Note* in the *Telephone* section under *How to Apply*, later.
• The ZIP code for EIN Operations at the Philadelphia Internal Revenue Service Center now includes a ZIP+4 extension. The revised ZIP code is 19255-0525.
• The Fax-TIN number for EIN Operations at the Philadelphia Internal Revenue Service Center has changed to 1-267-941-1040. See the *Where to File or Fax* table on page 2.

Federal tax deposits must be made by electronic funds transfer. Beginning January 1, 2011, you must use electronic funds transfer to make all federal tax deposits (such as deposits of employment tax, excise tax, and corporate income tax). Forms 8109 and 8109-B, Federal Tax Deposit Coupon, cannot be used after December 31, 2010. Generally, electronic fund transfers are made using the Electronic Federal Tax Payment System (EFTPS). If you do not want to use EFTPS, you can arrange for your tax professional, financial institution, payroll service, or other trusted third party to make deposits on your behalf. You also may arrange for your financial institution to initiate a same-day wire on your behalf. EFTPS is a free service provided by the Department of Treasury. Services provided by your tax professional, financial institution, payroll service, or other third party may have a fee.

To get more information about EFTPS or to enroll in EFTPS, visit *www.eftps.gov* or call 1-800-555-4477. Additional information about EFTPS is also available in Publication 966, The Secure Way to Pay Your Federal Taxes.

General Instructions

Use these instructions to complete Form SS-4, Application for Employer Identification Number (EIN). Also see *Do I Need an EIN?* on page 2 of Form SS-4.

Purpose of Form

Use Form SS-4 to apply for an EIN. An EIN is a nine-digit number (for example, 12-3456789) assigned to sole proprietors, corporations, partnerships, estates, trusts, and other entities for tax filing and reporting purposes. The information you provide on this form will establish your business tax account.

 An EIN is for use in connection with your business activities only. Do not use your EIN in place of your social security number (SSN).

Reminders

Apply online. Generally, you can apply for and receive an EIN on IRS.gov. See *How To Apply*, later.

 This is a free service offered by the Internal Revenue Service at IRS.gov.

File only one Form SS-4. Generally, a sole proprietor should file only one Form SS-4 and needs only one EIN, regardless of

the number of businesses operated as a sole proprietorship or trade names under which a business operates. However, if a sole proprietorship incorporates or enters into a partnership, a new EIN is required. Also, each corporation in an affiliated group must have its own EIN.

EIN applied for, but not received. If you do not have an EIN by the time a return is due, write "Applied For" and the date you applied in the space shown for the number. Do not show your SSN as an EIN on returns.

If you do not have an EIN by the time a tax deposit is due, send your payment to the Internal Revenue Service Center for your filing area as shown in the instructions for the form that you are filing. Make your check or money order payable to the "United States Treasury" and show your name (as shown on Form SS-4), address, type of tax, period covered, and date you applied for an EIN.

Election to file Form 944. Eligible employers may now elect to file Form 944 annually instead of Forms 941 quarterly. See *Line 14. Do you want to file Form 944?* on page 5 for details.

Electronic filing and payment. Businesses can file and pay federal taxes electronically. Use e-file and the Electronic Federal Tax Payment System (EFTPS).
• For additional information about e-file, visit IRS.gov.
• For additional information about EFTPS, visit *www.eftps.gov* or call EFTPS Customer Service at 1-800-555-4477, 1-800-733-4829 (TDD), or 1-800-244-4829 (Spanish).

Federal tax deposits. New employers that have a federal tax obligation will be pre-enrolled in EFTPS. EFTPS allows you to make all of your federal tax payments online at *www.eftps.gov* or by telephone. Shortly after we have assigned you your EIN, you will receive instructions by mail for activating your EFTPS enrollment. You will also receive an EFTPS Personal Identification Number (PIN) that you will use when making your payments, as well as instructions for obtaining an online password.

For more information on federal tax deposits, see Pub. 15 (Circular E), Employer's Tax Guide.

How To Apply

You can apply for an EIN online, by telephone, by fax, or by mail, depending on how soon you need to use the EIN. Use only one method for each entity so you do not receive more than one EIN for an entity.

Online. Taxpayers and authorized third party designees located within the United States and U.S. possessions can receive an EIN online and use it immediately to file a return or make a payment. Go to the IRS website at *www.irs.gov/businesses* and click on *Employer ID Numbers*.

 Taxpayers who apply online have an option to view, print, and save their EIN assignment notice at the end of the session. (Authorized third party designees will receive the EIN, however, the EIN assignment notice will be mailed to the applicant.)

 Applicants who are not located within the United States or U.S. possessions cannot use the online application to obtain an EIN. Please use one of the other methods to apply.

Telephone. You can receive your EIN by telephone and use it immediately to file a return or make a payment. Call the IRS at 1-800-829-4933 (toll free). The hours of operation are 7:00 a.m. to 10:00 p.m. local time (Pacific time for Alaska and Hawaii).

Cat. No. 62736F

The person making the call must be authorized to sign the form or be an authorized designee. See *Third Party Designee* and *Signature* on page 6. Also see the first *TIP* on page 2.

Note. International applicants must call 1-267-941-1099 (not toll free).

If you are applying by telephone, it will be helpful to complete Form SS-4 before contacting the IRS. An IRS representative will use the information from the Form SS-4 to establish your account and assign you an EIN. Write the number you are given on the upper right corner of the form and sign and date it. Keep this copy for your records.

If requested by an IRS representative, mail or fax the signed Form SS-4 (including any third party designee authorization) within 24 hours to the IRS address provided by the IRS representative.

 *Taxpayer representatives can apply for an EIN on behalf of their client and request that the EIN be faxed to their client on the same day. **Note.** By using this procedure, you are authorizing the IRS to fax the EIN without a cover sheet.*

Fax. Under the Fax-TIN program, you can receive your EIN by fax within 4 business days. Complete and fax Form SS-4 to the IRS using the appropriate Fax-TIN number listed below. A long-distance charge to callers outside of the local calling area will apply. Fax-TIN numbers can only be used to apply for an EIN. The numbers may change without notice. Fax-TIN is available 24 hours a day, 7 days a week.

Be sure to provide your fax number so the IRS can fax the EIN back to you.

Mail. Complete Form SS-4 at least 4 to 5 weeks before you will need an EIN. Sign and date the application and mail it to the service center address for your state. You will receive your EIN in the mail in approximately 4 weeks. Also see *Third Party Designee* on page 6.

Call 1-800-829-4933 to verify a number or to ask about the status of an application by mail.

 Form SS-4 downloaded from IRS.gov is a fill-in form, and when completed, is suitable for faxing or mailing to the IRS.

Where to File or Fax

If your principal business, office or agency, or legal residence in the case of an individual, is located in:	File or fax with the "Internal Revenue Service Center" at:
One of the 50 states or the District of Columbia	Attn: EIN Operation Cincinnati, OH 45999 Fax-TIN: 859-669-5760
If you have no legal residence, principal place of business, or principal office or agency in any state or the District of Columbia:	Attn: EIN Operation Philadelphia, PA 19255-0525 Fax-TIN: 267-941-1040

How To Get Forms and Publications

Internet. You can download, view, and order tax forms, instructions, and publications at IRS.gov.

Phone. Call 1-800-TAX-FORM (1-800-829-3676) to order forms, instructions, and publications. You should receive your order or notification of its status within 10 workdays.

DVD for Tax Products. For small businesses, return preparers, or others who may frequently need tax forms or publications, a DVD containing over 2,000 tax products (including many prior year forms) can be purchased from the National Technical Information Service (NTIS).

To order Pub. 1796, IRS Tax Products DVD, call 1-877-233-6767 or go to *www.irs.gov/cdorders*.

 Tax help for your business is available at www.irs.gov/businesses/*.

Related Forms and Publications

The following forms and instructions may be useful to filers of Form SS-4.
● Form 11-C, Occupational Tax and Registration Return for Wagering.
● Form 637, Application for Registration (For Certain Excise Tax Activities).
● Form 720, Quarterly Federal Excise Tax Return.
● Form 730, Monthly Tax Return for Wagers.
● Form 941, Employer's QUARTERLY Federal Tax Return.
● Form 944, Employer's ANNUAL Federal Tax Return.
● Form 990-T, Exempt Organization Business Income Tax Return.
● Instructions for Form 990-T.
● Form 1023, Application for Recognition of Exemption Under Section 501(c)(3) of the Internal Revenue Code.
● Form 1024, Application for Recognition of Exemption Under Section 501(a).
● Schedule C (Form 1040), Profit or Loss From Business (Sole Proprietorship).
● Schedule F (Form 1040), Profit or Loss From Farming.
● Instructions for Form 1041 and Schedules A, B, G, J, and K-1, U.S. Income Tax Return for Estates and Trusts.
● Form 1042, Annual Withholding Tax Return for U.S. Source Income of Foreign Persons.
● Instructions for Form 1065, U.S. Return of Partnership Income.
● Instructions for Form 1066, U.S. Real Estate Mortgage Investment Conduit (REMIC) Income Tax Return.
● Instructions for Forms 1120.
● Form 2290, Heavy Highway Vehicle Use Tax Return.
● Form 2553, Election by a Small Business Corporation.
● Form 2848, Power of Attorney and Declaration of Representative.
● Form 8821, Tax Information Authorization.
● Form 8832, Entity Classification Election.
● Form 8849, Claim for Refund of Excise Taxes.

For more information about filing Form SS-4 and related issues, see:
● Pub. 15 (Circular E), Employer's Tax Guide;
● Pub. 51 (Circular A), Agricultural Employer's Tax Guide;
● Pub. 538, Accounting Periods and Methods;
● Pub. 542, Corporations;
● Pub. 557, Tax-Exempt Status for Your Organization;
● Pub. 583, Starting a Business and Keeping Records;
● Pub. 966, The Secure Way to Pay Your Federal Taxes for Business and Individual Taxpayers;
● Pub. 1635, Understanding Your EIN.

Specific Instructions

Follow the instructions for each line to expedite processing and to avoid unnecessary IRS requests for additional information. Enter "N/A" on the lines that do not apply.

Line 1. Legal name of entity (or individual) for whom the EIN is being requested. Enter the legal name of the entity (or individual) applying for the EIN exactly as it appears on the social security card, charter, or other applicable legal document. An entry is required.

Individuals. Enter your first name, middle initial, and last name. If you are a sole proprietor, enter your individual name, not your business name. Enter your business name on line 2. Do not use abbreviations or nicknames on line 1.

Trusts. Enter the name of the trust as it appears on the trust instrument.

Estate of a decedent. Enter the name of the estate. For an estate that has no legal name, enter the name of the decedent followed by "Estate."

Partnerships. Enter the legal name of the partnership as it appears in the partnership agreement.

Corporations. Enter the corporate name as it appears in the corporate charter or other legal document creating it.

Plan administrators. Enter the name of the plan administrator. A plan administrator who already has an EIN should use that number.

Line 2. Trade name of business. Enter the trade name of the business if different from the legal name. The trade name is the "doing business as" (DBA) name.

 Use the full legal name shown on line 1 on all tax returns filed for the entity. (However, if you enter a trade name on line 2 and choose to use the trade name instead of the legal name, enter the trade name on all returns you file.) To prevent processing delays and errors, use only the legal name (or the trade name) on all tax returns.

Line 3. Executor, administrator, trustee, "care of" name. For trusts, enter the name of the trustee. For estates, enter the name of the executor, administrator, or other fiduciary. If the entity applying has a designated person to receive tax information, enter that person's name as the "care of" person. Enter the individual's first name, middle initial, and last name.

Lines 4a–b. Mailing address. Enter the mailing address for the entity's correspondence. If the entity's address is outside the United States or its possessions, you must enter the city, province or state, postal code, and the name of the country. Do not abbreviate the country name. If line 3 is completed, enter the address for the executor, trustee or "care of" person. Generally, this address will be used on all tax returns.

If the entity is filing the Form SS-4 only to obtain an EIN for the Form 8832, use the same address where you would like to have the acceptance or nonacceptance letter sent.

TIP *File Form 8822, Change of Address, to report any subsequent changes to the entity's mailing address.*

Lines 5a–b. Street address. Provide the entity's physical address only if different from its mailing address shown in lines 4a–b. Do not enter a P.O. box number here. If the entity's address is outside the United States or its possessions, you must enter the city, province or state, postal code, and the name of the country. Do not abbreviate the country name.

Line 6. County and state where principal business is located. Enter the entity's primary physical location.

Lines 7a–b. Name of responsible party. Enter the full name (first name, middle initial, last name, if applicable) and SSN, ITIN (individual taxpayer identification number), or EIN of the entity's responsible party as defined below.

Responsible party defined. For entities with shares or interests traded on a public exchange, or which are registered with the Securities and Exchange Commission, "responsible party" is (a) the principal officer, if the business is a corporation, (b) a general partner, if a partnership, (c) the owner of an entity that is disregarded as separate from its owner (disregarded entities owned by a corporation enter the corporation's name and EIN), or (d) a grantor, owner, or trustor, if a trust.

For all other entities, "responsible party" is the person who has a level of control over, or entitlement to, the funds or assets in the entity that, as a practical matter, enables the individual, directly or indirectly, to control, manage, or direct the entity and the disposition of its funds and assets. The ability to fund the entity or the entitlement to the property of the entity alone, however, without any corresponding authority to control, manage, or direct the entity (such as in the case of a minor child beneficiary), does not cause the individual to be a responsible party.

If the person in question is an alien individual with a previously assigned ITIN, enter the ITIN in the space provided and submit a copy of an official identifying document. If necessary, complete Form W-7, Application for IRS Individual Taxpayer Identification Number, to obtain an ITIN.

You must enter an SSN, ITIN, or EIN on line 7b unless the only reason you are applying for an EIN is to make an entity classification election (see Regulations sections 301.7701-1 through 301.7701-3) and you are a nonresident alien or other foreign entity with no effectively connected income from sources within the United States.

Lines 8a–c. Limited liability company (LLC) information. An LLC is an entity organized under the laws of a state or foreign country as a limited liability company. For federal tax purposes, an LLC may be treated as a partnership or corporation or be disregarded as an entity separate from its owner.

By default, a domestic LLC with only one member is disregarded as an entity separate from its owner and must include all of its income and expenses on the owner's tax return (for example, Schedule C (Form 1040)). Also by default, a domestic LLC with two or more members is treated as a partnership. A domestic LLC may file Form 8832 to avoid either default classification and elect to be classified as an association taxable as a corporation. For more information on entity classifications (including the rules for foreign entities), see the instructions for Form 8832.

If the answer to line 8a is "Yes," enter the number of LLC members. If the LLC is owned solely by a husband and wife in a community property state and the husband and wife choose to treat the entity as a disregarded entity, enter "1" on line 8b.

 Do not file Form 8832 if the LLC accepts the default classifications above. If the LLC is eligible to be treated as a corporation that meets certain tests and it will be electing S corporation status, it must timely file Form 2553. The LLC will be treated as a corporation as of the effective date of the S corporation election and does not need to file Form 8832. See the Instructions for Form 2553.

Line 9a. Type of entity. Check the box that best describes the type of entity applying for the EIN. If you are an alien individual with an ITIN previously assigned to you, enter the ITIN in place of a requested SSN.

⚠ *This is not an election for a tax classification of an entity. See Disregarded entities on page 4.*

Sole proprietor. Check this box if you file Schedule C, or Schedule F (Form 1040) and have a qualified plan, or are required to file excise, employment, alcohol, tobacco, or firearms returns, or are a payer of gambling winnings. Enter your SSN (or ITIN) in the space provided. If you are a nonresident alien with no effectively connected income from sources within the United States, you do not need to enter an SSN or ITIN.

Corporation. This box is for any corporation other than a personal service corporation. If you check this box, enter the income tax form number to be filed by the entity in the space provided.

⚠ *If you entered "1120S" after the "Corporation" checkbox, the corporation must file Form 2553 no later than the 15th day of the 3rd month of the tax year the election is to take effect. Until Form 2553 has been received and approved, you will be considered a Form 1120 filer. See the Instructions for Form 2553.*

Personal service corporation. Check this box if the entity is a personal service corporation. An entity is a personal service corporation for a tax year only if:
• The principal activity of the entity during the testing period (prior tax year) for the tax year is the performance of personal services substantially by employee-owners, and
• The employee-owners own at least 10% of the fair market value of the outstanding stock in the entity on the last day of the testing period.

Personal services include performance of services in such fields as health, law, accounting, or consulting. For more

Instr. for Form SS-4 (2011)   -3-

information about personal service corporations, see the Instructions for Form 1120 and Pub. 542.

 If the corporation is recently formed, the testing period begins on the first day of its tax year and ends on the earlier of the last day of its tax year, or the last day of the calendar year in which its tax year begins.

Other nonprofit organization. Check this box if the nonprofit organization is other than a church or church-controlled organization and specify the type of nonprofit organization (for example, an educational organization).

 If the organization also seeks tax-exempt status, you must file either Form 1023 or Form 1024. See Pub. 557 for more information.

If the organization is covered by a group exemption letter, enter the four-digit group exemption number (GEN) in the last entry. (Do not confuse the GEN with the nine-digit EIN.) If you do not know the GEN, contact the parent organization. See Pub. 557 for more information about group exemption letters.

If the organization is a section 527 political organization, check the box for *Other nonprofit organization* and specify "section 527 organization" in the space to the right. To be recognized as exempt from tax, a section 527 political organization must electronically file Form 8871, Political Organization Notice of Section 527 Status, within 24 hours of the date on which the organization was established. The organization may also have to file Form 8872, Political Organization Report of Contributions and Expenditures. See *www.irs.gov/polorgs* for more information.

Plan administrator. If the plan administrator is an individual, enter the plan administrator's taxpayer identification number (TIN) in the space provided.

REMIC. Check this box if the entity has elected to be treated as a real estate mortgage investment conduit (REMIC). See the Instructions for Form 1066 for more information.

State/local government. If you are a government employer and you are not sure of your social security and Medicare coverage options, go to *www.ncsssa.org/statessadminmenu.html* to obtain the contact information for your state's Social Security Administrator.

Other. If not specifically listed, check the "Other" box, enter the type of entity and the type of return, if any, that will be filed (for example, "Common Trust Fund, Form 1065" or "Created a Pension Plan"). Do not enter "N/A." If you are an alien individual applying for an EIN, see the *Lines 7a–b* instructions on page 3.
- **Household employer.** If you are an individual that will employ someone to provide services in your household, check the "Other" box and enter "Household Employer" and your SSN. If you are a trust that qualifies as a household employer, you do not need a separate EIN for reporting tax information relating to household employees; use the EIN of the trust.
- **Household employer agent.** If you are an agent of a household employer that is a disabled individual or other welfare recipient receiving home care services through a state or local program, check the "Other" box and enter "Household Employer Agent." (See Rev. Proc. 80-4, 1980-1 C.B. 581; Rev. Proc. 84-33, 1984-1 C.B. 502; and Notice 2003-70, 2003-43 I.R.B. 916.) If you are a state or local government also check the box for state/local government.
- **QSub.** For a qualified subchapter S subsidiary (QSub) check the "Other" box and specify "QSub."
- **Withholding agent.** If you are a withholding agent required to file Form 1042, check the "Other" box and enter "Withholding Agent."

Disregarded entities. A disregarded entity is an eligible entity that is disregarded as separate from its owner for federal income tax purposes. Disregarded entities include single-member limited liability companies (LLCs) that are disregarded as separate from their owners, qualified subchapter S subsidiaries (qualified subsidiaries of an S corporation), and certain qualified foreign entities. See the Instructions for Form 8832 and Regulations section 301.7701-3 for more information on domestic and foreign disregarded entities.

For wages paid on or after January 1, 2009, the disregarded entity is required to use its name and EIN for reporting and payment of employment taxes. A disregarded entity is also required to use its name and EIN to register for excise tax activities on Form 637, pay and report excise taxes reported on Forms 720, 730, 2290, and 11-C, and claim any refunds, credits, and payments on Form 8849. See the instructions for the employment and excise tax returns for more information.

Complete Form SS-4 for disregarded entities as follows.
- If a disregarded entity is filing Form SS-4 to obtain an EIN because it is required to report and pay employment and excise taxes (see above) or for non-federal purposes such as a state requirement, check the "Other" box for line 9a and write "disregarded entity" (or "disregarded entity-sole proprietorship" if the owner of the disregarded entity is an individual).
- If the disregarded entity is requesting an EIN for purposes of filing Form 8832 to elect classification as an association taxable as a corporation, or Form 2553 to elect S corporation status, check the "Corporation" box for line 9a and write "single-member" and the form number of the return that will be filed (Form 1120 or 1120S).
- If the disregarded entity is requesting an EIN because it has acquired one or more additional owners and its classification has changed to partnership under the default rules of Regulations section 301.7701-3(f), check the "Partnership" box for line 9a.

Line 10. Reason for applying. Check only one box. Do not enter "N/A." A selection is required.

Started new business. Check this box if you are starting a new business that requires an EIN. If you check this box, enter the type of business being started. Do not apply if you already have an EIN and are only adding another place of business.

Hired employees. Check this box if the existing business is requesting an EIN because it has hired or is hiring employees and is therefore required to file employment tax returns. Do not apply if you already have an EIN and are only hiring employees. For information on employment taxes (for example, for family members), see Pub. 15 (Circular E).

 You must make electronic deposits of all depository taxes (such as employment tax, excise tax, and corporate income tax) using EFTPS. See Federal tax deposits must be made by electronic funds transfer on page 1; section 11, Depositing Taxes, in Pub. 15 (Circular E); and Pub. 966.

Banking purpose. Check this box if you are requesting an EIN for banking purposes only, and enter the banking purpose (for example, a bowling league for depositing dues or an investment club for dividend and interest reporting).

Changed type of organization. Check this box if the business is changing its type of organization. For example, the business was a sole proprietorship and has been incorporated or has become a partnership. If you check this box, specify in the space provided (including available space immediately below) the type of change made. For example, "From Sole Proprietorship to Partnership."

Purchased going business. Check this box if you purchased an existing business. Do not use the former owner's EIN unless you became the "owner" of a corporation by acquiring its stock.

Created a trust. Check this box if you created a trust, and enter the type of trust created. For example, indicate if the trust is a nonexempt charitable trust or a split-interest trust.

Exception. Do not file this form for certain grantor-type trusts. The trustee does not need an EIN for the trust if the trustee furnishes the name and TIN of the grantor/owner and the address of the trust to all payers. However, grantor trusts that do not file using Optional Method 1 and IRA trusts that are required to file Form 990-T, Exempt Organization Business Income Tax Return, must have an EIN. For more information on grantor trusts, see the Instructions for Form 1041.

 Do not check this box if you are applying for a trust EIN when a new pension plan is established. Check "Created a pension plan."

-4-

Instr. for Form SS-4 (2011)

Created a pension plan. Check this box if you have created a pension plan and need an EIN for reporting purposes. Also, enter the type of plan in the space provided.

 Check this box if you are applying for a trust EIN when a new pension plan is established. In addition, check the "Other" box on line 9a and write "Created a Pension Plan" in the space provided.

Other. Check this box if you are requesting an EIN for any other reason; and enter the reason. For example, a newly-formed state government entity should enter "Newly-Formed State Government Entity" in the space provided.

Line 11. Date business started or acquired. If you are starting a new business, enter the starting date of the business. If the business you acquired is already operating, enter the date you acquired the business. For foreign applicants, this is the date you began or acquired a business in the United States. If you are changing the form of ownership of your business, enter the date the new ownership entity began. Trusts should enter the date the trust was funded. Estates should enter the date of death of the decedent whose name appears on line 1 or the date when the estate was legally funded.

Line 12. Closing month of accounting year. Enter the last month of your accounting year or tax year. An accounting or tax year is usually 12 consecutive months, either a calendar year or a fiscal year (including a period of 52 or 53 weeks). A calendar year is 12 consecutive months ending on December 31. A fiscal year is either 12 consecutive months ending on the last day of any month other than December or a 52-53 week year. For more information on accounting periods, see Pub. 538.

Individuals. Your tax year generally will be a calendar year.

Partnerships. Partnerships must adopt one of the following tax years.
- The tax year of the majority of its partners.
- The tax year common to all of its principal partners.
- The tax year that results in the least aggregate deferral of income.
- In certain cases, some other tax year.

See the Instructions for Form 1065 for more information.

REMICs. REMICs must have a calendar year as their tax year.

Personal service corporations. A personal service corporation generally must adopt a calendar year unless it meets one of the following requirements.
- It can establish a business purpose for having a different tax year.
- It elects under section 444 to have a tax year other than a calendar year.

Trusts. Generally, a trust must adopt a calendar year except for the following trusts.
- Tax-exempt trusts.
- Charitable trusts.
- Grantor-owned trusts.

Line 13. Highest number of employees expected in the next 12 months. Complete each box by entering the number (including zero ("-0-")) of "Agricultural," "Household," or "Other" employees expected by the applicant in the next 12 months.

If no employees are expected, skip line 14.

Line 14. Do you want to file Form 944? If you expect your employment tax liability to be $1,000 or less in a full calendar year, you are eligible to file Form 944 annually (once each year) instead of filing Form 941 quarterly (every three months). Your employment tax liability generally will be $1,000 or less if you expect to pay $4,000 or less in total wages subject to social security and Medicare taxes and federal income tax withholding. If you qualify and want to file Form 944 instead of Forms 941, check the box on line 14. If you do not check the box, then you must file Form 941 for every quarter.

 For employers in the U.S. possessions, generally, if you pay $6,536 or less in wages subject to social security and Medicare taxes, you are likely to pay $1,000 or less in employment taxes.

For more information on employment taxes, see Pub. 15 (Circular E); or Pub. 51 (Circular A) if you have agricultural employees (farmworkers).

Line 15. First date wages or annuities were paid. If the business has employees, enter the date on which the business began to pay wages or annuities. For foreign applicants, this is the date you began to pay wages in the United States. If the business does not plan to have employees, enter "N/A."

Withholding agent. Enter the date you began or will begin to pay income (including annuities) to a nonresident alien. This also applies to individuals who are required to file Form 1042 to report alimony paid to a nonresident alien. For foreign applicants, this is the date you began or will begin to pay income (including annuities) to a nonresident alien in the United States.

Line 16. Check the one box on line 16 that best describes the principal activity of the applicant's business. Check the "Other" box (and specify the applicant's principal activity) if none of the listed boxes applies. You must check a box.

Construction. Check this box if the applicant is engaged in erecting buildings or engineering projects (for example, streets, highways, bridges, tunnels). The term "Construction" also includes special trade contractors (for example, plumbing, HVAC, electrical, carpentry, concrete, excavation, etc. contractors).

Real estate. Check this box if the applicant is engaged in renting or leasing real estate to others; managing, selling, buying, or renting real estate for others; or providing related real estate services (for example, appraisal services). Also check this box for mortgage real estate investment trusts (REITs). Mortgage REITs are engaged in issuing shares of funds consisting primarily of portfolios of real estate mortgage assets with gross income of the trust solely derived from interest earned.

Rental and leasing. Check this box if the applicant is engaged in providing tangible goods such as autos, computers, consumer goods, or industrial machinery and equipment to customers in return for a periodic rental or lease payment. Also check this box for equity real estate investment trusts (REITs). Equity REITs are engaged in issuing shares of funds consisting primarily of portfolios of real estate assets with gross income of the trust derived from renting real property.

Manufacturing. Check this box if the applicant is engaged in the mechanical, physical, or chemical transformation of materials, substances, or components into new products. The assembling of component parts of manufactured products is also considered to be manufacturing.

Transportation & warehousing. Check this box if the applicant provides transportation of passengers or cargo; warehousing or storage of goods; scenic or sight-seeing transportation; or support activities related to transportation.

Finance & insurance. Check this box if the applicant is engaged in transactions involving the creation, liquidation, or change of ownership of financial assets and/or facilitating such financial transactions; underwriting annuities/insurance policies; facilitating such underwriting by selling insurance policies; or by providing other insurance or employee-benefit related services.

Health care & social assistance. Check this box if the applicant is engaged in providing physical, medical, or psychiatric care or providing social assistance activities such as youth centers, adoption agencies, individual/family services, temporary shelters, daycare, etc.

Accommodation & food services. Check this box if the applicant is engaged in providing customers with lodging, meal preparation, snacks, or beverages for immediate consumption.

Wholesale–agent/broker. Check this box if the applicant is engaged in arranging for the purchase or sale of goods owned by others or purchasing goods on a commission basis for goods traded in the wholesale market, usually between businesses.

Wholesale–other. Check this box if the applicant is engaged in selling goods in the wholesale market generally to other businesses for resale on their own account, goods used in production, or capital or durable nonconsumer goods.

Retail. Check this box if the applicant is engaged in selling merchandise to the general public from a fixed store; by direct, mail-order, or electronic sales; or by using vending machines.

Other. Check this box if the applicant is engaged in an activity not described above. Describe the applicant's principal business activity in the space provided.

Line 17. Use line 17 to describe the applicant's principal line of business in more detail. For example, if you checked the "Construction" box on line 16, enter additional detail such as "General contractor for residential buildings" on line 17. An entry is required. For mortgage REITs indicate mortgage REIT and for equity REITs indicate what type of real property is the principal type (residential REIT, nonresidential REIT, miniwarehouse REIT).

Line 18. Check the applicable box to indicate whether or not the applicant entity applying for an EIN was issued one previously.

Third Party Designee. Complete this section only if you want to authorize the named individual to receive the entity's EIN and answer questions about the completion of Form SS-4. The designee's authority terminates at the time the EIN is assigned and released to the designee. You must complete the signature area for the authorization to be valid.

Signature. When required, the application must be signed by (a) the individual, if the applicant is an individual, (b) the president, vice president, or other principal officer, if the applicant is a corporation, (c) a responsible and duly authorized member or officer having knowledge of its affairs, if the applicant is a partnership, government entity, or other unincorporated organization, or (d) the fiduciary, if the applicant is a trust or an estate. Foreign applicants may have any duly-authorized person (for example, division manager) sign Form SS-4.

Privacy Act and Paperwork Reduction Act Notice. We ask for the information on this form to carry out the Internal Revenue laws of the United States. We need it to comply with section 6109 and the regulations thereunder, which generally require the inclusion of an employer identification number (EIN) on certain returns, statements, or other documents filed with the Internal Revenue Service. If your entity is required to obtain an EIN, you are required to provide all of the information requested on this form. Information on this form may be used to determine which federal tax returns you are required to file and to provide you with related forms and publications.

We disclose this form to the Social Security Administration (SSA) for their use in determining compliance with applicable laws. We may give this information to the Department of Justice for use in civil and/or criminal litigation, and to cities, states, the District of Columbia, and U.S. commonwealths and possessions for use in administering their tax laws. We may also disclose this information to other countries under a tax treaty, to federal and state agencies to enforce federal nontax criminal laws, and to federal law enforcement and intelligence agencies to combat terrorism.

We will be unable to issue an EIN to you unless you provide all of the requested information that applies to your entity. Providing false information could subject you to penalties.

You are not required to provide the information requested on a form that is subject to the Paperwork Reduction Act unless the form displays a valid OMB control number. Books or records relating to a form or its instructions must be retained as long as their contents may become material in the administration of any Internal Revenue law. Generally, tax returns and return information are confidential, as required by section 6103.

The time needed to complete and file this form will vary depending on individual circumstances. The estimated average time is:

Recordkeeping	8 hrs., 36 min.
Learning about the law or the form	42 min.
Preparing, copying, assembling, and sending the form to the IRS	52 min.

If you have comments concerning the accuracy of these time estimates or suggestions for making this form simpler, we would be happy to hear from you. You can write to Internal Revenue Service, Tax Products Coordinating Committee, SE:W:CAR:MP:T:T:SP, IR-6526, 1111 Constitution Avenue, NW, Washington, DC 20224. Do not send the form to this address. Instead, see *Where to File or Fax* on page 2.

Instr. for Form SS-4 (2011)

Note: Form SS-4 begins on the next page of this document.

Attention

Limit of five (5) Employer Identification Number (EIN) Assignments per Business Day

Due to a high volume of requests for EINs, the IRS will begin limiting the number

of EINs assigned per day to a responsible party identified on Form SS-4.

Effective April 11, 2011, a responsible party will be limited to **five (5) EINs** in one

business day. This limit is in effect whether you apply online, by phone, fax, or

mail.

Form **SS-4** (Rev. January 2010) Department of the Treasury Internal Revenue Service	**Application for Employer Identification Number** **(For use by employers, corporations, partnerships, trusts, estates, churches,** **government agencies, Indian tribal entities, certain individuals, and others.)** ▶ **See separate instructions for each line.** ▶ **Keep a copy for your records.**	OMB No. 1545-0003 EIN

	1 Legal name of entity (or individual) for whom the EIN is being requested	

	2 Trade name of business (if different from name on line 1)	**3** Executor, administrator, trustee, "care of" name
Type or print clearly.	**4a** Mailing address (room, apt., suite no. and street, or P.O. box)	**5a** Street address (if different) (Do not enter a P.O. box.)
	4b City, state, and ZIP code (if foreign, see instructions)	**5b** City, state, and ZIP code (if foreign, see instructions)
	6 County and state where principal business is located	
	7a Name of responsible party	**7b** SSN, ITIN, or EIN

8a	Is this application for a limited liability company (LLC) (or a foreign equivalent)? . . . . ☐ **Yes** ☐ **No**	**8b** If 8a is "Yes," enter the number of LLC members . . . . . ▶
8c	If 8a is "Yes," was the LLC organized in the United States? . . . . ☐ **Yes** ☐ **No**	

9a Type of entity (check only one box). **Caution.** If 8a is "Yes," see the instructions for the correct box to check.

☐ Sole proprietor (SSN) _____ : _____ : _____
☐ Partnership
☐ Corporation (enter form number to be filed) ▶_____
☐ Personal service corporation
☐ Church or church-controlled organization
☐ Other nonprofit organization (specify) ▶_____
☐ Other (specify) ▶

☐ Estate (SSN of decedent) _____ : _____
☐ Plan administrator (TIN) _____
☐ Trust (TIN of grantor) _____
☐ National Guard   ☐ State/local government
☐ Farmers' cooperative   ☐ Federal government/military
☐ REMIC   ☐ Indian tribal governments/enterprises
Group Exemption Number (GEN) if any ▶

9b	If a corporation, name the state or foreign country (if applicable) where incorporated	State	Foreign country

10 **Reason for applying** (check only one box)

☐ Started new business (specify type) ▶ _____
☐ Hired employees (Check the box and see line 13.)
☐ Compliance with IRS withholding regulations
☐ Other (specify) ▶

☐ Banking purpose (specify purpose) ▶_____
☐ Changed type of organization (specify new type) ▶_____
☐ Purchased going business
☐ Created a trust (specify type) ▶_____
☐ Created a pension plan (specify type) ▶_____

11 Date business started or acquired (month, day, year). See instructions.	**12** Closing month of accounting year
13 Highest number of employees expected in the next 12 months (enter -0- if none). If no employees expected, skip line 14.	**14** If you expect your employment tax liability to be $1,000 or less in a full calendar year **and** want to file Form 944 annually instead of Forms 941 quarterly, check here. (Your employment tax liability generally will be $1,000 or less if you expect to pay $4,000 or less in total wages.) If you do not check this box, you must file Form 941 for every quarter. ☐

Agricultural	Household	Other

15 First date wages or annuities were paid (month, day, year). **Note.** If applicant is a withholding agent, enter date income will first be paid to nonresident alien (month, day, year) . . . . ▶

16 Check **one** box that best describes the principal activity of your business.
☐ Construction ☐ Rental & leasing ☐ Transportation & warehousing
☐ Real estate ☐ Manufacturing ☐ Finance & insurance
☐ Health care & social assistance ☐ Wholesale-agent/broker
☐ Accommodation & food service ☐ Wholesale-other ☐ Retail
☐ Other (specify)

17 Indicate principal line of merchandise sold, specific construction work done, products produced, or services provided.

18 Has the applicant entity shown on line 1 ever applied for and received an EIN? ☐ **Yes** ☐ **No**
If "Yes," write previous EIN here ▶

Third Party Designee	Complete this section **only** if you want to authorize the named individual to receive the entity's EIN and answer questions about the completion of this form.	
	Designee's name	Designee's telephone number (include area code) ( )
	Address and ZIP code	Designee's fax number (include area code) ( )

Under penalties of perjury, I declare that I have examined this application, and to the best of my knowledge and belief, it is true, correct, and complete.

Name and title (type or print clearly) ▶

Signature ▶   Date ▶

Applicant's telephone number (include area code)
(   )
Applicant's fax number (include area code)
(   )

For Privacy Act and Paperwork Reduction Act Notice, see separate instructions.   Cat. No. 16055N   Form **SS-4** (Rev. 1-2010)

Do I Need an EIN?

File Form SS-4 if the applicant entity does not already have an EIN but is required to show an EIN on any return, statement, or other document.[1] See also the separate instructions for each line on Form SS-4.

IF the applicant...	AND...	THEN...
Started a new business	Does not currently have (nor expect to have) employees	Complete lines 1, 2, 4a–8a, 8b–c (if applicable), 9a, 9b (if applicable), and 10–14 and 16–18.
Hired (or will hire) employees, including household employees	Does not already have an EIN	Complete lines 1, 2, 4a–6, 7a–b (if applicable), 8a, 8b–c (if applicable), 9a, 9b (if applicable), 10–18.
Opened a bank account	Needs an EIN for banking purposes only	Complete lines 1–5b, 7a–b (if applicable), 8a, 8b–c (if applicable), 9a, 9b (if applicable), 10, and 18.
Changed type of organization	Either the legal character of the organization or its ownership changed (for example, you incorporate a sole proprietorship or form a partnership) [2]	Complete lines 1–18 (as applicable).
Purchased a going business [3]	Does not already have an EIN	Complete lines 1–18 (as applicable).
Created a trust	The trust is other than a grantor trust or an IRA trust [4]	Complete lines 1–18 (as applicable).
Created a pension plan as a plan administrator [5]	Needs an EIN for reporting purposes	Complete lines 1, 3, 4a–5b, 9a, 10, and 18.
Is a foreign person needing an EIN to comply with IRS withholding regulations	Needs an EIN to complete a Form W-8 (other than Form W-8ECI), avoid withholding on portfolio assets, or claim tax treaty benefits [6]	Complete lines 1–5b, 7a–b (SSN or ITIN optional), 8a, 8b–c (if applicable), 9a, 9b (if applicable), 10, and 18.
Is administering an estate	Needs an EIN to report estate income on Form 1041	Complete lines 1–6, 9a, 10–12, 13–17 (if applicable), and 18.
Is a withholding agent for taxes on non-wage income paid to an alien (i.e., individual, corporation, or partnership, etc.)	Is an agent, broker, fiduciary, manager, tenant, or spouse who is required to file Form 1042, Annual Withholding Tax Return for U.S. Source Income of Foreign Persons	Complete lines 1, 2, 3 (if applicable), 4a–5b, 7a–b (if applicable), 8a, 8b–c (if applicable), 9a, 9b (if applicable), 10, and 18.
Is a state or local agency	Serves as a tax reporting agent for public assistance recipients under Rev. Proc. 80-4, 1980-1 C.B. 581 [7]	Complete lines 1, 2, 4a–5b, 9a, 10, and 18.
Is a single-member LLC	Needs an EIN to file Form 8832, Classification Election, for filing employment tax returns and excise tax returns, or for state reporting purposes [8]	Complete lines 1–18 (as applicable).
Is an S corporation	Needs an EIN to file Form 2553, Election by a Small Business Corporation [9]	Complete lines 1–18 (as applicable).

[1] For example, a sole proprietorship or self-employed farmer who establishes a qualified retirement plan, or is required to file excise, employment, alcohol, tobacco, or firearms returns, must have an EIN. A partnership, corporation, REMIC (real estate mortgage investment conduit), nonprofit organization (church, club, etc.), or farmers' cooperative must use an EIN for any tax-related purpose even if the entity does not have employees.

[2] However, do not apply for a new EIN if the existing entity only (a) changed its business name, (b) elected on Form 8832 to change the way it is taxed (or is covered by the default rules), or (c) terminated its partnership status because at least 50% of the total interests in partnership capital and profits were sold or exchanged within a 12-month period. The EIN of the terminated partnership should continue to be used. See Regulations section 301.6109-1(d)(2)(iii).

[3] Do not use the EIN of the prior business unless you became the "owner" of a corporation by acquiring its stock.

[4] However, grantor trusts that do not file using Optional Method 1 and IRA trusts that are required to file Form 990-T, Exempt Organization Business Income Tax Return, must have an EIN. For more information on grantor trusts, see the Instructions for Form 1041.

[5] A plan administrator is the person or group of persons specified as the administrator by the instrument under which the plan is operated.

[6] Entities applying to be a Qualified Intermediary (QI) need a QI-EIN even if they already have an EIN. See Rev. Proc. 2000-12.

[7] See also *Household employer* on page 4 of the instructions. **Note.** State or local agencies may need an EIN for other reasons, for example, hired employees.

[8] See *Disregarded entities* on page 4 of the instructions for details on completing Form SS-4 for an LLC.

[9] An existing corporation that is electing or revoking S corporation status should use its previously-assigned EIN.

To Obtain 501(c)(3) Tax Exempt Status

Submit IRS Form 1023, Application for Recognition of Exemption to:

> Internal Revenue Service
> Post Office Box 192
> Covington, KY 41012-0192
> Telephone: 877-829-5500 Questions/Information
> Telephone: 800-829-3676 Forms
> Web: www.irs.gov/charities

Filing fee: $850, or $400 if the organization's revenues are less than $10,000 annually.

IRS Form 1023 can be found here:
http://www.irs.gov/pub/irs-pdf/f1023.pdf.

Instructions for filling out IRS Form 1023 can be found here:
http://www.irs.gov/pub/irs-pdf/i1023.pdf.

ALABAMA

To apply for incorporation:

> Secretary of State
> Corporate Section
> Post Office Box 5616
> Montgomery, AL 36130-5616
> Telephone: 334-242-5324
> Web: www.sos.alabama.gov/businessservices/DomesticCorps.aspx

For your convenience, the state provides blank Articles of Incorporation, along with easy-to-follow instructions. The forms can be found at: www.sos.alabama.gov/downloads/corpForms.aspx.

The first step is to obtain a name reservation from the Secretary of State for the name you have chosen for your organization. The next step is to file the completed Articles of Incorporation at the Judge of Probate office in the county where the organization's principal office will be located. You will need to include two copies of the articles, along with a copy of the name reservation form.

In Alabama, it is not necessary for nonprofit organizations to include the word Incorporated or Corporation (or the like) in the name.

Filing fees:

The filing fee for the Judge of Probate is $50 and the Secretary of State fee is $100. You will remit both fees to the Judge of Probate. You may expedite the process by paying an additional $100 fee.

Alabama does require exempt organizations to file an annual state information report. Organizations are required to renew their registration with a financial report, and pay the $25 fee within 90 days of their year-end. IRS Form 990 can be substituted for the financial report.

Alabama does not have a general exemption for nonprofit organizations for property and sales and use taxes. There are some organization types that by legislative act, have been granted exemption. To find out how this affects your organization, please contact the Alabama Department of Revenue.

Taxes:

> Alabama Department of Revenue
> Corporate Section
> Post Office Box 327430
> Montgomery, AL 36132-7430
> Telephone: (334) 242-1170
> Web: www.ador.state.al.us

Charitable Solicitation registration:

> Office of the Attorney General
> Consumer Protection Section
> Attn: Charitable Organization Registration
> Post Office Box 300152
> Montgomery, AL 36130
>
> Filing fee: $25

ALASKA

To apply for incorporation:

> Department of Commerce and Economic Development
> Division of Corporations, Business, and Professional Licensing
> Post Office Box 110806
> Juneau, AK 99811-0806
> Telephone: 907-465-2550
> Email: corporations@alaska.gov
> Web: www.dced.state.ak.us/occ/home_corporations.html

Naming requirements:

To reserve a name, the state provides the following form: http://www.dced.state.ak.us/occ/pub_corp/08-580.pdf.

There is a $25 fee for a 120-day reservation.

To register your organization's chosen name, the state requires the completion of the following form: http://www.dced.state.ak.us/occ/pub_corp/08-575.pdf.

The fee to register your organization's name is $25.

The state of Alaska provides user-friendly forms and easy-to-complete Articles of Incorporation. The website includes instructions, as well as other important information for charitable organizations operating in Alaska.

The form requires the disclosure of at least three initial members of the organization's board of directors. The filing fee is $50 and is payable to the Alaska Department of Commerce and Economic Development.

Taxes:

> Alaska Department of Revenue
> Post Office Box 110420
> Juneau, AK 99811-0420
> Telephone: (907) 465-2320
> FAX: (907) 465-2375
> Web: www.revenue.state.ak.us/

Alaska requires nonprofit organizations to file a biennial report with a due date of July 2, every other year. A late fee will be incurred for reports postmarked after August 1. You may call the Corporations section with any questions at (907) 465-2550. Don't forget to keep a copy of the report if submitting online.

Organizations are able to file the report online at: https://www.commerce. state.ak.us/CBP/CorporationLicensing/CorpFormIntro.aspx?FormId=-7105.

Charitable Solicitation registration:

> State of Alaska
> Department of Law
> Attorney General's Office
> 1031 West 4th, Suite 200
> Anchorage, AK 99501-5200

The deadline to file the registration documentation is September 1 of each year. The filing fee is $40. Annual filing is required and there are some exemptions for you to review.

ARIZONA

To apply for incorporation:

> Arizona Corporation Commission
> 1300 W. Washington, 1st Floor
> Phoenix, AZ 85007-2929
> Telephone: 602-542-3026
> Telephone: 800-345-5819 (in state only)

> Or

> 400 W. Congress, 2nd Floor
> Tucson, AZ 85701
> Telephone: 520-628-6560
> Web: www.cc.state.az.us/

The state of Arizona provides online access to Articles of Incorporation, Certificates of Disclosure, and Cover Sheets to aid in the filing of the required documents.

Within 60 days of the acceptance of your Articles of Incorporation, a copy of the document must be published in the newspaper with general circulation in the county of the organization. It must run in three consecutive publications including the document. A list of qualified newspapers will be provided by the state and is also available at www.azcc.gov/divisions/corporations.

The filing fee is $40 and is payable to the Arizona Corporation Commission. For expedited service, add an additional $35.

Naming requirements:

You can call the Commission at (602) 542-3135, to check your corporate name prior to completing the request document. To reserve your organization's proposed name electronically, the state of Arizona provides the following electronic document: http://starpas.azcc.gov/scripts/cgiip.exe/WService=wsbroker1/eforms.p?form-number=CF0059.

Other filing options:

> Arizona Corporation Commission
> Corporate Filings Section
> 1300 W. Washington
> Phoenix, AZ 85007
> FAX: (602) 542-4100

A name can be reserved for 120 days for a fee of $10. For expedited service, the fee is $45.

Taxes:

> Department of Revenue
> Corporate Section
> 600 W. Monroe
> Phoenix, AZ 85007
> Telephone: (602) 255-3381
> FAX: (602) 542-2072
> Web: www.azdor.gov
>
> Tax Returns
> Post Office Box 29079
> Phoenix, AZ 85038-9079

The state of Arizona requires annual reporting for all corporations.

Charitable Solicitation registration:

> Secretary of State
> Attn: Business Services, Charities Division
> 1700 West Washington, 7th Floor
> Phoenix, AZ 85007-2888
> Telephone: (602) 542-6187
> Web: www.azsos.gov

Exemptions from registration exist and filing is required annually.

ARKANSAS

To apply for incorporation:

> Arkansas Secretary of State
> Business and Commercial Services
> 1401 W. Capitol Avenue, Suite 250
> Victory Building
> Little Rock, AR 72201
> Telephone: 501-682-3409
> Web: www.sos.arkansas.gov

The Arkansas Secretary of State provides fill-in-the-blank documents in online and PDF formats. The filing fees for the Articles of Incorporation are $45 for online processing and $50 for paper or hardcopy filings. Checks should be made payable to the Secretary of State.

Annual reports must be filed by August 1 each year.

Taxes:

> Department of Finance and Administration
> 7th and Wolfe
> Post Office Box 1272
> Little Rock, AR 72203-0919
> Telephone: (501) 682-4779
> FAX: (501) 682-7900
> Web: www.dfa.arkansas.gov

Charitable Solicitation registration:

> Office of the Attorney General
> Consumer Protection Division
> 323 Center Street, Suite 200
> Little Rock, AR 72201
> Telephone: (501) 682-1109 or (800) 482-8982

Annual filings are required. Some exemptions are available.

CALIFORNIA

To apply for incorporation:

> Office of the Secretary of State
> Business Programs Division
> 1500 11th Street, 3rd Floor
> Sacramento, CA 95814
> Telephone: 916-657-5448

> Or

> 300 South Spring Street, Room 12513
> Los Angeles, CA 90013
> Web: www.sos.ca.gov/business

Online Articles of Incorporation: http://www.sos.ca.gov/business/corp/pdf/articles/corp_artsnp.pdf.

The filing fee is $30, with an additional $15 for expedited services or the special handling of documents that are delivered to their office in person.

You will be required to file an annual report, which is due by the 15th of the 5th month following the organization's year-end close.

Taxes:

> Franchise Tax Board
> Exempt Organizations Unit, MS F120
> Post Office Box 1286
> Rancho Cordova, CA 95741-1286
> Telephone: (916) 845-4171

> Or

> Post Office Box 942857
> Sacramento, CA 94257
> Telephone: (800) 852-5711
> Web: www.ftb.ca.gov

FTB 3500 Exemption Application should be mailed to:

> Franchise Tax Board
> Post Office Box 942857
> Sacramento, CA 94257

Charitable Solicitations registration:

> Registry of Charitable Trust
> Post Office Box 903447
> Sacramento, CA 94203-4470
> Telephone: (916) 445-2021
> Web: www.ag.ca.gov/charities

Organizations with revenue of less than $25,000 are exempt from registration. The fee is revenue based and ranges from $25 to $300. Organizations that are not exempt must file annually.

COLORADO

To apply for incorporation:

> Secretary of State
> Corporations Office
> 1700 Broadway
> Denver, CO 80290
> Telephone: (303) 894-2200, ext 6487
> FAX: (303) 894-4871
> Email: charitable@sos.state.co.us
> Web: http://www.sos.state.co.us/pubs/charities/charitableHome.html

All corporate filings are completed online after creating a free account. Easy-to-complete fill-in-the-blank Articles of Incorporation are provided for your convenience.

The registration filing and annual renewal is $10. Credit cards are accepted.

Annual corporate reports are required with a due date of the 15th of the 5th month following the organization's year-end close.

Taxes:

> Department of Revenue
> Taxpayer Service Division
> 1375 Sherman Street
> Denver, CO 80261
> Telephone: (303) 238-7378
> Web: www.colorado.gov/cs/satellite/revenue/REVX/1176842266433

Charitable Solicitation registration:

> Secretary of State
> 1560 Broadway, 2nd Floor
> Denver, CO 80202
> Telephone: (303) 894-2200
> Web: http://www.sos.state.co.us/pubs/charities/charitableHome.html

There are no exemptions, but the online form is easy to fill out and there are no associated fees.

CONNECTICUT

To apply for incorporation:

> Secretary of State
> 30 Trinity Street
> Post Office Box 150470
> Hartford, CT 06115-0470
> Telephone: (860) 509-6002
> Web: www.sots.ct.gov/sots/site/default.asp

The filing fee for a Domestic Non-stock Corporation Certificate of Incorporation is $50. Expedited service is available for an additional $50.

To reserve a corporate name, the filing fee is $60. The name will be reserved for 120 days.

Both forms are available on the following web page: http://www.sots.ct.gov/sots/cwp/view.asp?a=3177&q=472426#corp.

Annual filings are required, beginning January 1, 2012, it is mandatory to file the reports online.

Taxes:

> Department of Revenue Services
> 25 Sigourney Street, Suite 2
> Hartford, CT 06106-5032
> Telephone: (860) 297-5962
> FAX: (203) 297-5714
> Web: www.ct.gov/drs/site/default.asp

Nonprofit corporations receive an automatic exemption once status is approved by the IRS.

Charitable Solicitations registration:

> Attorney General
> Public Charities Unit
> 165 Capitol Avenue
> Hartford, CT 06106-1630
> Telephone: (860) 713-6170
> Web: www.ct.gov/ag/cwp/browse.asp?a=2074
> Email: ctcharityhelp@ct.gov

There are a few exemptions available, primarily less than $25,000 annual revenue and no paid fundraiser. The registration fee is $50 and is payable to the Treasurer, State of Connecticut.

DELAWARE

To apply for incorporation:

> State of Delaware
> Division of Corporations
> Post Office Box 898
> Dover, DE 19903

> Or

> 401 Federal Street, Suite 4
> Dover, DE 19901
> Telephone: (302) 739-3073
> Web: www.sos.delaware.gov

Helpful forms and information are provided at the following web address: www.corp.delaware.gov/Inc_Exempt.pdf.

Name reservations can be made by calling (302) 739-3073. The name will be reserved for 30 days with a $75 fee, payable to Delaware Secretary of State.

The filing fee for nonprofit organizations is $89, plus $9 per page after the first page. Expedited services are available and are as follows:

> Priority Services (1–2 hours) range from $500 to $1,000
> Same-day Service is available for an additional $100
> 24-hour Service is available for an additional $50

Annual reports are required and the filing fee is $50.

Taxes:

> Department of Finance
> Division of Revenue
> Carvel State Office Building
> 820 North French Street
> Wilmington, DE 19801
> Telephone: (302) 577-8200
> FAX: (302) 577-8202
> Web: www.revenue.delaware.gov

There is no automatic exemption.

Charitable Solicitation registration:

> Attorney General
> Civil Division
> Carvel State Office Building
> 820 N. French Street
> Wilmington, DE 19801
> Telephone: (302) 577-8400

The state of Delaware has no statute requiring registration.

DISTRICT OF COLUMBIA

To apply for incorporation:

Department of Consumer and Regulatory Affairs
Corporations Division
Post Office Box 92300
Washington, DC 20090

Or

1100 4th Street, SW
Washington, DC 20024
Telephone: (202) 442-4400
FAX: (202) 442-4523
Web: http://dcra.dc.gov
Email: dcra@dc.gov

The filing fees are $77, payable to the DC Treasurer. Expedited services are available:

Same-day Service—add $100
3-day Service—add $50

Annual reports are required.

Taxes:

Office of Tax and Revenue
1101 4th Street SW, Suite W270
Washington, DC 20024
Telephone: (202) 727-4TAX
FAX: (202) 727-6304
Web: http://otr.cfo.dc.gov/otr/site/default.asp

There is no automatic exemption.

Charitable Solicitation registration:

> Department of Consumer and Regulatory Affairs
> 614 H Street, NW
> Washington, DC 20001
> Telephone: (202) 442-4432

Annual filing is required.

FLORIDA

To apply for incorporation:

> Florida Department of State
> Division of Corporations
> Post Office Box 6327
> Tallahassee, FL 32314
> Telephone: (904) 245-6052
> FAX: (904) 487-6052
> Email: corphelp@dos.state.fl.us
> Web: www.sunbiz.org

Excellent website with sample Articles of Incorporation. There must be three directors and the principal place of business MUST be a street address.

The filing fee is $70, payable to the Department of State. For an additional $8.75, you may receive a Certified Copy.

Annual reports are required and are due between January 1 and May 1. The filing fee is $61.25 and the report is filed online at www.sunbiz.org.

To reserve a name, you can check availability at www.sunbiz.org. The reservation fee is $35 and the name will be reserved for 120 days.

Taxes:

> Florida Department of Revenue
> 5050 West Tennessee Street
> Tallahassee, FL 32399-0100
> Telephone: (800) 352-3671
> Web: http://dor.myflorida.com/dor/
> Email: emaildor@dor.state.fl.us

Charitable Solicitation registration:

> Department of Agriculture and Consumer Services
> Division of Consumer Services
> Post Office Box 6700
> Tallahassee, FL 32399-6700
> Telephone: (850) 488-2221 or (800) 435-7352
> FAX: (850) 921-8201
> Web: www.freshfromflorida.com/onestop/forms/10100.pdf

Some exemptions are available; filing fees range from $10 to $400 and are payable to FDACS.

GEORGIA

To apply for incorporation:

> Secretary of State
> 2 Martin Luther King, Jr. Drive
> Suite 313, West Tower
> Atlanta, GA 30334-1530
> Telephone: (404) 656-2817
> Web: www.sos.ga.gov/corporations

Names can be reserved by calling (404) 656-2817 or at www.georgiacorporations.org. The fee is $25, payable to the Office of Secretary of State. The reservation will last for 30 days.

The filing fee for the corporation is $60, payable to the Secretary of State. Georgia does require annual reports to be filed.

Taxes:

> Georgia Taxpayer Services Division
> Tax Exempt Organizations
> 1800 Century Boulevard NE, Suite 15311
> Atlanta, GA 30345
> Telephone: (404) 417-6649
> FAX: (404) 417-2101

Form 3605 is no longer required.

Charitable Solicitation registration:

> Secretary of State
> Professional Licensing Boards
> Securities Division
> 237 Coliseum Drive
> Macon, GA 31217-3858
> Telephone: (478) 207-2440
> Web: http://www.sos.state.ga.us/securities/

The initial filing fee is $35; annual renewal fee is $20. Checks should be made payable to Georgia Secretary of State.

HAWAII

To apply for incorporation:

> Department of Commerce and Consumer Affairs
> Business Registration Division
> 1010 Richards Street
> Post Office Box 40
> Honolulu, HI 96810
> Telephone: 808-586-2727
> FAX: 808-586-2722
> Web: http://hawaii.gov/dcaa

For your convenience, the state of Hawaii provides fill-in-the-blank Articles of Incorporation (Form DNP-1).

To register your corporation's name, the state charges a $10 fee. It is easy to create an online account to file and retrieve documents. The filing fee is $25 to file the DNP-1; checks should be made payable to the Department of Commerce and Consumer Affairs.

The state of Hawaii requires the filing of annual reports, based on the date of the initial filing. A fee of $5 is charged upon submission of the report.

To register for Charitable Solicitation:

> Department of the Attorney General
> Tax Division/Charities Unit
> 425 Queens Street
> Honolulu, HI 96813
> Telephone: 808-586-1480
> FAX: 808-586-8116
> Web: http://hawaii.gov/ag/charities

A wonderful online tutorial can be found under the frequently asked question section at: www.hawaii.gov/ag/charities/416657_1.pdf.

The Office of the Attorney General requires most nonprofit corporations to submit an annual copy of the organization's 990. The annual filing fee ranges from $10 to $600, based on the organization's annual gross revenues.

IDAHO

To apply for incorporation:

> Office of the Secretary of State
> 450 North 4th Street
> Post Office Box 83720
> Boise, ID 83720-0080
> Telephone: 208-334-2301
> FAX: 208-334-2080
> Web: www.sos.idaho.gov

The state of Idaho provides both printable and fill-in-the-blank Articles of Incorporation forms on the Secretary of State's website. The direct web address is: http://www.sos.idaho.gov/corp/acro4/arts_inc_np.pdf.

To reserve your chosen corporate name, the fee is $20 and provides a four-month reservation period. You can pay an additional $20 for expedited service. To register your corporation and file your Articles of Incorporation, the filing fee is $30, payable to the Secretary of State. Just like with the name reservation, you can pay an additional $20 for expedited service.

Reports:

The state of Idaho does require annual reports, but does not charge a fee.

Taxes:

> State Tax Commission
> Department of Revenue and Taxation
> Post Office Box 36
> Boise, ID 83772-0410
> Telephone: 208-334-7660
> Web: http://tax.idaho.gov/

To register for Charitable Solicitation:

State of Idaho
Attorney General
Business Regulation Division
700 West Jefferson, Suite 210
Post Office Box 83720
Boise, ID 83720-0010
Telephone: 208-334-2400
FAX: 208-854-8071
Web: www.ag.idaho.gov

ILLINOIS

To apply for incorporation:

> Secretary of State
> Business Services Department
> Michael J. Howlett Building
> 501 S. 2nd Street, Room 350
> Springfield, IL 62756
> Telephone: 217-782-6961 (general information)
> Telephone: 217-782-9520 (organization name availability)

> Or

> 69 West Washington, Suite1240
> Chicago, IL 60602
> Telephone: 312-793-3380
> Web: www.sos.state.il.us

The state of Idaho provides fill-in-the-blank Articles of Incorporation at: http://www.sos.idaho.gov/corp/acro4/arts_inc_np.pdf.

The filing fee for the registration and filing of the Articles of Incorporation is $50, payable to the Secretary of State. You may add an additional $25 for expedited services. Idaho also charges a payment processing fee of $2.75. To reserve your chosen corporate name, the state charges a fee of $25, payable to the Secretary of State. For your convenience, complete online Form NFP 104.10.

Reports:

The state requires an annual report, which is due within six months of the organization's calendar or fiscal year-end.

Taxes:

> Illinois Department of Revenue
> Income Tax Division
> Willard Ice Building
> 101 West Jefferson Street
> Springfield, IL 62702
> Telephone: 217-782-3336

> Or

James R. Thompson Center
100 West Randolph
Concourse Level
Chicago, IL 60601-3274
Telephone: 800-732-8866
Web: http://www.revenue.state.il.us/nonprofits/index.htm

Charitable Solicitation registration:

Attorney General
Charitable Trust Division
100 West Randolph
Chicago, IL 60601
Telephone: 312-814-3000

Or

500 South Second Street
Springfield, IL 62706
Telephone: 217-782-1090

The state charges a filing fee of $15 to register. The check should be made payable to the Illinois Charity Bureau Fund. Corporations with gross revenues of less than $15,000 may file the simplified report.

INDIANA

To apply for incorporation:

>Secretary of State
>302 West Washington, Room E018
>Indianapolis, IN 46204
>Telephone: 317-232-6576 or
>Telephone: 317-232-6581
>FAX: 317-233-3387
>Web: www.in.gov/sos/business/3672.htm

Indiana's Secretary of State provides an Adobe document that can be completed and printed for submission of the organization's Articles of Incorporation. You will submit one original set of documents and one copy to the address above, if filing by mail. The filing fee is $30 for hard-copy submissions or $20 for online filing.

Annual reports are required by the state. The annual report filing fee is $10 for mailed submissions or $5 for online report submissions.

Taxes:

>Indiana Department of Revenue
>Tax Administration
>Post Office Box 7147
>Indianapolis, IN46207-7147
>Telephone: 317-233-4015
>Web: www.in.gov/dor

To file for an exemption, you will complete application Form NP-20A. The annual required report is NP-20.

Charitable Solicitation registration:

>Attorney General
>Consumer Protection Division
>Indiana Government Center South
>302 West Washington, 5th Floor
>Indianapolis, IN 46204
>Telephone: 317-232-6330 or
>Telephone: 800-382-5516
>Web: www.in.gov/attorneygeneral/index.htm

The state of Indiana does not currently require registration of charitable organizations.

IOWA

To apply for incorporation:

> Secretary of State
> Business Services
> First Floor, Lucas Building
> 321 East 12th Street
> Des Moines, IA 50319
> Telephone: 515-281-5204
> FAX: 515-242-5953
> Web: http://www.sos.state.ia.us/business/nonprofits/index.html

The Secretary of State's website provides a wealth of information. The filing fee for registering your organization is $20, payable to the Secretary of State. There is also a name reservation fee of $10.

There are annual reporting requirements, but there is no fee associated with the report.

Taxes:

> Iowa Department of Revenue
> Business Section
> Hoover Office Building, 4th Floor
> 1305 East Walnut
> Des Moines, IA 50319
> Telephone: 515-281-3114
> FAX: 515-242-6487
> Web: www.iowa.gov

Charitable Solicitation registration:

> Attorney General
> Consumer Protection Division
> 1300 East Walnut
> Hoover State Building
> Des Moines, IA 50319
> Telephone: 515-281-5926
> Email: consumer@ag.state.ia.us

The registration form is found at: http://www.state.ia.us/government/ag/consumer/credit_code_forms/charitfinancialformweb.pdf.

KANSAS

To apply for incorporation:

> Kansas Office of the Secretary of State
> Corporation Division
> Memorial Hall, 1st Floor
> 120 SW 10th Avenue
> Topeka, KS 66612-1594
> Telephone: 785-296-4564
> Web: www.sos.ks.gov

The state provides a printable Articles of Incorporation form for your filing convenience. There is a filing fee of $20, payable to the Secretary of State for submission of Form 17-6002. The form is available at: www.kssos.org/forms/business_services/CN.pdf.

Kansas requires nonprofit organizations to file an annual report with a filing fee of $40.

Taxes:

> Kansas Department of Revenue
> Docking State Office Building
> 915 SW Harrison Street (at 10th and Harrison)
> Topeka, KS 66625
> Telephone: 785-296-3081
> FAX: 785-291-3614
> Web: www.ksrevenue.org

The state of Kansas provides an automatic exemption once the IRS awards its determination.

Charitable Solicitation registration:

> Kansas Office of the Secretary of State
> Corporation Division
> Memorial Hall, 1st Floor
> 120 SW 10th Avenue
> Topeka, KS 66612-1594
> Telephone: 785-296-4564
> Web: www.sos.ks.gov

The state requires an annual filing of the Statement for Solicitations, with a fee of $35.

KENTUCKY

To apply for incorporation:

> Commonwealth of Kentucky
> Office of the Secretary of State
> 700 Capitol Avenue, Suite 154
> Post Office Box 718
> Frankfort, KY 40601
> Telephone: 502-564-2848
> Web: www.sos.ky.gov

The Commonwealth provides a sample Articles of Incorporation, but unfortunately while the outline satisfies the state's requirements, they do not satisfy the IRS's. You should strongly consider using the samples provided elsewhere. The filing fee is a reasonable $8, payable to the Secretary of State.

An annual report is due each June, with a filing fee of $15.

To verify the availability of your chosen name, you may call 502-564-3490. A name reservation can be made for a fee of $15 (payable to the Kentucky State Treasurer) and is valid for a period of 120 days.

Taxes:

> Commonwealth of Kentucky
> Revenue Cabinet
> 501 High Street
> Frankfort, KY 40620
> Telephone: 502-564-8139
> Web: www.revenue.ky.gov/business

Charitable Solicitation registration:

> Attorney General
> Division of Consumer Protection
> 700 Capitol Avenue, Suite 118
> Frankfort, KY 40601-3449
> Telephone: 888-432-9257 or
> Telephone: 502-696-5389

The Commonwealth of Kentucky allows for the use of the Unified Registration Statement (URS) or the organization's most recent IRS Form 990 for the initial filing, as well as the subsequent annual filings.

LOUISIANA

To apply for incorporation:

> Louisiana Secretary of State
> Corporations Division
> Post Office Box 94125
> Baton Rouge, LA 70804-9125

> Or

> Twelve United Plaza
> 8585 Archives Avenue
> Baton Rouge, LA 70809
> Telephone: 225-925-4704
> FAX: 225-932-5314
> Web: www.sos.la.gov

The state of Louisiana's Secretary of State's website provides Article of Incorporation forms for printing and mailing, as well as forms for online submissions. The printable form can be found at: http://www.sos.la.gov/Portals/0/395ArticlesofIncorporationLouisianaNonProfit.pdf. The filing fee is $60, payable to the Secretary of State. You may add an additional $30 for 24-hour processing. To reserve your chosen name, the filing fee is $25.

Louisiana requires an annual report, with a filing fee of $5.

Taxes:

> Department of Revenue
> 617 North Third Street
> Baton Rouge, LA 70802

Or

> Post Office Box 201
> Baton Rouge, LA 70821
> Telephone: 225-219-7462
> Web: www.rev.state.la.us/

The state of Louisiana provides an automatic exemption for nonprofit organizations.

Charitable Solicitation registration:

> Attorney General
> Public Protection Division
> 1885 North Third Street, 4th Floor
> Baton Rouge, LA 70802
> Telephone: 225-326-6400
> FAX: 225-326-6499
> Web: www.ag.louisiana.gov

Louisiana's initial registration requires more documentation than many other states (likely a result of the recent natural disasters and the explosion of charitable organizations in their state). The fee for the initial registration and annual renewal is $25. In addition to the filing fee, the documents required for the initial application include the Unified Registration Statement (URS), a copy of the Articles of Incorporation, a copy of the organization's bylaws, a copy of the IRS Determination Letter, and the most recent IRS Form 990. The requirements found on the Attorney General's website are clear and easy to follow.

MAINE

To apply for incorporation:

Office of the Secretary of State
Bureau of Corporations, Elections, and Commissions
Division of Corporations
101 State House Station
Augusta, ME 04333-0101
Telephone: 207-624-7752
Email: cec.corporations@maine.gov
Web: http://www.maine.gov/sos/cec/corp/NonprofitResources.html

The state provides a fill-in-the-blank printable form, which is located at: http://www.maine.gov/sos/cec/corp/formsnew/mnpca6.pdf. The filing fees include a name reservation fee of $5 and a name registration fee of $5/month. The corporate filing fee is $40, payable to the Secretary of State. For immediate service, you may add an additional $100 fee. Maine also provides a 24-hour expedited service for an additional fee of $50.

Maine does require annual reporting, which can be printed and mailed or submitted online. The filing fee is $35.

Taxes:

Department of Finance and Administration
Bureau of Taxation
78 State House Station
Augusta, ME 04333
Telephone: 207-624-7800
FAX: 207-624-7804
Web: www.maine.gov/dafs/

The state does provide an automatic exemption for organizations that have received their IRS Determination Letter. You must complete an application for exemption from sales tax, with a filing fee of $25. For more information, please follow this link: http://www.state.me.us/revenue/salesuse/exmptindex.html.

Charitable Solicitation registration:

> State of Maine
> Department of Professional and Financial Regulation
> Office of Licensing and Registration
> 35 State House Station
> Augusta, ME 04333
> Telephone: 207-624-8603
> FAX: 207-624-8637
> Web: http://www.maine.gov/pfr/professionallicensing/professions/
> charitable/organization.htm

The state charges a filing fee of $50, payable to the Maine State Treasurer. Maine does not accept the URS. The license expires annually on November 30. The renewal fee is $25. There is a late fee of $50 if you do not renew by the expiration date.

MARYLAND

To apply for incorporation:

> State Department of Assessments and Taxation
> Charter Room 801
> 301 West Preston Street
> Baltimore, MD 21201-2395
> Telephone: 410-767-1330
> Web: www.dat.state.md.us

The state provides forms that can be completed and mailed to the address above. All forms MUST be typed! The form is found at: http://www.dat.state.md.us/sdatweb/ex_corp_form.pdf. To file the Articles of Incorporation, the filing fee is $100, plus a $20 organization and capitalization fee and a $50 assessment for the Maryland Not-For-Profit Development Center Program Fund. In addition to the $170 total fee, you may add an additional $50 for expedited service.

The state requires the filing of annual reports. Form 1 is due April 15 each year and does not have a filing fee for domestic non-stock organizations.

Taxes:

> Comptroller of the Treasury
> Revenue Administration Division
> 110 Carroll Street
> Annapolis, MD 21411
> Telephone: 410-260-7980
> Web: www.comp.state.md.us

There is no automatic exemption. Ensure that you review their website for the required filings.

Charitable Solicitation registration:

> Office of the Secretary of State
> Charitable Organization Division
> State House
> Annapolis, MD 21401
> Telephone: 410-974-5534

Organizations must complete the Registration Statement, Form COR-92. The associated fee is based on the organization's level of charitable contributions and ranges from $0 to $200. The check should be payable to the Secretary of State.

MASSACHUSETTS

To apply for incorporation:

> Secretary of the Commonwealth
> One Ashburton Place, 17th Floor
> Boston, MA 02108
> Telephone: 617-727-9640
> Email: corpinfo@sec.state.ma.us
> Web: http://www.sec.state.ma.us

The state provides a large amount of useful information, including sample Articles of Incorporation. The Secretary of State's website offers access to required forms for nonprofit organizations at: http://www.sec.state.ma.us/cor/corpweb/cornp/npfrm.htm. The filing fee is $35 and should be made payable to the Commonwealth of Massachusetts.

To verify if your chosen organizational name is available, you may call 617-727-9640. The reservation fee is $30 and must be submitted by mail or in person.

The Commonwealth requires charitable organizations to file annual reports by November 1 of each year. The filing fee is $15.

Taxes:

> Department of Revenue
> Customer Service Bureau
> Post Office Box 7010
> Boston, MA 02204
> Telephone: 617-887-6367 or
> Telephone: 800-392-6089 (in state)
> Web: www.mass.gov

The state does not provide for automatic exemption.

Charitable Solicitation registration:

> Office of the Attorney General
> Non-Profit Organizations/Public Charities Division
> One Ashburton Place
> Boston, MA 02108
> Telephone: 617-727-2200, extension 2101
> Web: http://www.mass.gov/ago/doing-business-in-massachusetts/public-charities-or-not-for-profits/

The Attorney General requires annual filings and accepts the URS. The initial filing fee is $100, payable to the Commonwealth of Massachusetts. The form is found at the following link: http://www.sec.state.ma.us/cor/cor-pdf/180npcar.pdf.

MICHIGAN

To apply for incorporation:

>Michigan Department of Energy, Labor, and Economic Growth
>Bureau of Commercial Services
>Corporation Division
>7150 Harris Drive
>Post Office Box 30054
>Lansing, MI 48909
>Telephone: 888-767-6424
>Web: www.michigan.gov

The state provides an online form for completion and filing of the Articles of Incorporation. The form can be found at: http://www.michigan.gov/documents/CIS_Form_502_2457_7.pdf. The filing fee is $20, payable to the State of Michigan.

To verify the availability of your organization's chosen name, you may call 517-241-6470.

Michigan does require the filing of an annual report, along with a $20 filing fee payable to the State of Michigan. There are three ways you may file the report:

Online:

>www.michigan.gov/fileonline

In person:

>2501 Woodlake Circle
>Okemos, Michigan

By mail:

>Post Office Box 30767
>Lansing, MI 48909

Taxes:

>Department of the Treasury
>Bureau of Collections
>Lansing, MI 48922
>Telephone: 517-636-4700

The state does provide an automatic exemption from sales and use taxes.

Charitable Solicitation registration:

> Attorney General
> Charitable Trust Division
> Post Office Box 30214
> Lansing, MI 48909
> Telephone: 517-373-1152

Charitable organizations are required to file annually. There are currently no fees associated with this report. The initial application can be found at the following link: http://www.michigan.gov/documents/ag/Fillable_ Initial_App_2-9-09_266590_7.pdf. Check the instructions, as some organizations may be exempt from this requirement.

MINNESOTA

To apply for incorporation:

Minnesota Secretary of State
Division of Business Services
Retirement System of Minnesota Building
60 Empire Drive, Suite 100
St. Paul, MN 55103
Telephone: 651-296-2803
Web: www.sos.state.mn.us

The state provides sample Articles of Incorporation in PDF and Word formats. The filing fee is $70, payable to the Minnesota Secretary of State. Online Express Service is available for most filings for an additional $410.

The state requires an annual report and does not charge a fee for the filing.

You may check name availability online at: http://mblsportal.sos.state.mn.us. The fee to file for name reservation is $70, which includes the Express Service filing fee.

Taxes:

Minnesota Department of Revenue
600 North Robert Street
St. Paul, MN 55101
Telephone: 651-282-5225
Web: www.taxes.state.mn.us

The state does not have any automatic exemptions.

Charitable Solicitation registration:

Office of the Attorney General
Charities Division
1200 Bremer Tower
445 Minnesota Street
St. Paul, MN 55101-2130
Telephone: 651-757-1311

The initial and annual renewal is completed on the same document, found at the following address: http://www.ag.state.mn.us/Charities/Forms/ RegistrationAnnualReport.pdf. Both the initial filing and annual renewals will cost you $25. If you fail to complete the report in a timely manner, you will be charged a late fee of $50.

MISSISSIPPI

To apply for incorporation:

> Mississippi Secretary of State
> Business Services Division
> Post Office Box 136
> Jackson, MS 39205-0136
> Telephone: 601-359-1333
> FAX: 601-359-1607
> Web: www.sos.ms.gov

The state of Mississippi charges a filing fee of $50, payable to the Secretary of State, for processing your organization's Articles of Incorporation.

Taxes:

> Mississippi State Tax Commission
> Income and Franchise Tax Division
> Post Office Box 1033
> Jackson, MS 39125
> Telephone: 601-923-7000
> Web: http://www.dor.ms.gov/

The state does provide an automatic exemption upon filing of the appropriate form. There is no fee charged for this filing.

Charitable Solicitation registration:

> Mississippi Secretary of State
> Charities Registration
> Post Office Box 136
> Jackson, MS 39205-0136
> Telephone: 888-236-6167 or
> Telephone: 800-829-3676

There is a fee of $50 associated with the required filing of this registration.

MISSOURI

To apply for incorporation:

>Secretary of State
>Corporations Division
>Post Office Box 778
>Jefferson City, MO 65102
>
>Or
>
>600 W. Main Street
>Missouri State Information Center, Room 322
>Jefferson City, MO 65102
>Telephone: 866-223-6535
>FAX: 573-751-4153
>Email: corporations@sos.mo.gov
>Web: www.sos.mo.gov/business/corporations

The state provides a fill-in-the-blank Articles of Incorporation form at the following link: http://www.sos.mo.gov/forms/corp/corp52.pdf. The filing fee is $25, payable to the Director of Revenue.

You may call 573-751-3317 to verify the availability of your organization's chosen name. The state charges a fee of $25 to reserve the name.

An interesting option that the state of Missouri provides is a pre-examination. For a fee of $55, you may submit your completed forms for review to ensure completeness and accuracy.

Taxes:

>Missouri Department of Revenue
>Tax Clearance
>Post Office Box 3666
>Jefferson City, MO 65105-3666
>Telephone: 573-751-9268
>FAX: 573-522-1160
>Email: taxclearance@dor.mo.gov
>Web: http://www.dor.ms.gov/

Upon completion of DOR Form 943, charitable organizations receive an automatic exemption.

Charitable Solicitation registration:

Attorney General
Attn: Consumer Protection
Post Office Box 899
Jefferson, MO 65102
Telephone: 573-751-3321
Web: www.ago.mo.gov

The Attorney General of Missouri requires all charitable organizations that will solicit donations in their state to register and annually renew the registration. The filing fee for the initial registration, as well as the renewals, is $15.

MONTANA

To apply for incorporation:

> Montana Secretary of State
> State Capitol Building
> 1301 East 6th Avenue
> Helena, MT 59601

> or

> Post Office Box 202801
> Helena, MT 59620-2801
> Telephone: 406-444-3665
> FAX: 406-444-3976
> Email: secretary@mt.gov
> Web: www.sos.mt.gov

The state of Montana provides online fill-in-the-blank Articles of Incorporation at: www.sos.mt.gov/Business/Forms. The filing fee is $20, payable to the Secretary of State. For an additional $20, you will receive 24-hour processing and for an additional $100, you receive 1-hour processing.

An annual report is due by April 15 each year. The filing fee is $15 if filed on time. Reports submitted after the April 15 due date have a filing fee of $30.

To reserve the name you have chosen, the filing fee is $10 for 120 days. To register the name, the fee is $20. The state offers expedited service for an additional fee. As with the Articles of Incorporation, you may add an additional $20 to receive 24-hour service or an additional $100 to receive 1-hour processing.

Taxes:

> Montana Department of Revenue
> Attn: Certificates
> Post Office Box 5805
> Helena, MT 59604-5805
> Telephone: 406-444-6900
> FAX: 406-444-6642
> Email: DORTaxCertificates@mt.gov
> Web: www.revenue.mt.gov

The state does not provide an automatic exemption for charitable organizations.

Charitable Solicitation registration:

Attorney General
Montana Department of Justice
Consumer Protection
Post Office Box 201401
Helena, MT 59620-1401
Telephone: 406-444-2026
FAX: 406-444-3549
Email: contactdoj@mt.gov
Web: www.doj.mt.gov

There are currently no requirements for charitable organizations to register with the Attorney General's office.

NEBRASKA

To apply for incorporation:

> Secretary of State
> State Capitol Building
> 1445 K Street, Room 1301
> Lincoln, NE 68509
>
> Or
>
> Post Office Box 94608
> Lincoln, NE 68509-4608
> Telephone: 402-471-4079
> FAX: 402-471-3666
> Web: www.sos.ne.gov

The state of Nebraska does not provide blank Article of Incorporation forms in any format. You can easily use the information from the IRS's website. The filing fee is $10, plus $5 per page recording fee. The check should be payable to the Secretary of State.

Biennial reports are due to the Secretary of State by April 1 of odd-numbered years.

The fee to reserve the name you have chosen for your organization is $30 ($25, plus the $5 per page recording fee). The Secretary of State does provide a form for the name reservation.

Taxes:

> Department of Revenue
> Post Office Box 98903
> Lincoln, NE 68509-8903
> Telephone: 402-471-5729
> FAX: 402-471-5927
> Web: www.revenue.ne.gov

The state of Nebraska does provide an automatic exemption for charitable organizations.

Charitable Solicitation registration:

> Office of the Attorney General
> Consumer Protection Division
> 2115 State Capitol Building
> Lincoln, NE 68509
> Telephone: 402-471-2682
> Web: www.ago.state.ne.us

Currently, charitable organizations are not required to register with the Attorney General's office.

NEVADA

To apply for incorporation:

>Secretary of State
>204 North Carson Street, Suite 4
>Carson City, NV 89710
>Telephone: 775-684-5708
>FAX: 775-684-7138
>Web: www.nvsos.gov

The state of Nevada provides fill-in-the-blank Articles of Incorporation for your convenience. The form can be found at: http://nvsos.gov/Modules/ShowDocument.aspx?documentid=885. The filing fee is $50, with several expedite options. For an additional fee of $125, you can expect to receive 24-hour processing. If you need a faster turnaround, you can purchase 2-hour processing for an additional $500 or 1-hour processing for an additional $1,000! Certified copies will cost $30.

To reserve the organization's chosen name, you will need to pay $30 for a 90-day period. Check availability or get answers to your questions by calling 775-684-5708.

Your organization will be required to file an annual report, with the primary purpose of updating the list of officers and directors. The filing fee is $25.

Taxes:

>Department of Taxation
>1550 College Parkway, Suite 115
>Carson City, NV 89706
>Telephone: 775-684-2000
>FAX: 775-684-2020
>Web: www.tax.state.nv.us

The state of Nevada does not have a state income tax and provides an automatic exemption for charitable organizations.

Charitable Solicitation registration:

Nevada Department of Justice
Office of the Attorney General
100 North Carson Street
Carson City, NV 89701-4717
Telephone: 775-684-1100
Web: www.ag.state.nv.us

There are no current registration requirements for the state of Nevada.

NEW HAMPSHIRE

To apply for incorporation:

> Department of State
> Corporations Division
> State House Annex, Room 341
> 25 Capitol Street, 3rd Floor
> Concord, NH 03301-4989
> Telephone: 603-271-3246
> Email: corporate@sos.nh.gov
> Web: www.sos.nh.gov

The state of New Hampshire provides fill-in-the-blank Articles of Agreement. The filing fee for the city or town clerk is $5 and $25 for filing with the Secretary of State. Checks should be made payable to the State of New Hampshire.

New Hampshire requires the filing of "returns," beginning in 2010 and every five years thereafter, regardless of the incorporation date. The filing fee is $25. Please mail the return to:

> New Hampshire Department of State
> Annual Reports
> Post Office Box 9529
> Concord, NH 03108-9529
> Email: annualreports@sos.nh.gov

Taxes:

> Department of Revenue Administration
> 109 Pleasant Street
> Concord, NH 03301
> Telephone: 603-230-5000
> FAX: 603-271-6121
> Web: www.nh.gov/revenue

The state does provide for the automatic exemption for charitable organizations.

Charitable Solicitation registration:

Attorney General
Charitable Trusts Unit
33 Capitol Street
Concord, NH 03301
Telephone: 603-271-3591
Email: charitabletrusts@doj.nh.gov

The state requires the initial registration using Form NHCT-1, along with a $25 filing fee payable to the State of New Hampshire. Annual renewal reports are required 4 ½ months following the organization's year-end. The filing fee for the annual report (Form NHCT-2A) is $75. Failure to file an annual report is punishable by a fine up to $10,000.

NEW JERSEY

To apply for incorporation:

New Jersey Division of Revenue
Corporate Filing Unit
Post Office Box 308
Trenton, NJ 08646-0308

Or

225 West Slate Street, 3rd Floor
Trenton, NJ 08608-1001
Telephone: 609-292-9292
FAX: 609-984-6849
Web: www.state.nj.us/njbgs/

The filing fee is $75 for nonprofit organizations, payable to the Treasurer, State of New Jersey.

You may verify the availability of the name you have selected online free of charge. The reservation and/or registration fee is $50. You may choose to expedite service for a fee of $15. This provides 8 ½ business–hour processing.

Taxes:

New Jersey Regulatory Services Branch
Division of Taxation
Post Office Box 269
Trenton, NJ 08695-0269
Telephone: 609-292-5994
Web: www.state.nj.us/treasury/taxation

The state requires that charitable organizations file Form REG-1E. There is no automatic exemption.

Charitable Solicitation registration:

Charities Registration Section
New Jersey Division of Consumer Affairs
Post Office Box 45021
Newark, NJ 07101
Telephone: 973-504-6215
Email: askconsumeraffairs@lps.state.nj.us
Web: http://www.nj.gov/lps/ca/charity/charhlp.htm

Charitable organizations are required to register and renew annually.

NEW MEXICO

To apply for incorporation:

Public Regulation Commission
Corporations Bureau
Post Office Box 1269
1120 Paseo De Peralta
Santa Fe, NM 87501
Telephone: 505-827-4508
Telephone: 888-427-5772
FAX: 505-827-4387
Web: www.nmprc.state.nm.us/corporations

Articles of Incorporation are provided on the Public Regulation Commission's website or by following this link: http://www.nmprc.state.nm.us/corporations/pdf/charter/dnp.pdf. The filing fee is $25, payable to the New Mexico Public Regulation Commission (NMPRC). Name availability is checked when you file your registration online.

Annual reports are required by the state of New Mexico. The initial report is due within 30 days of the incorporation date. A penalty of $10 will be assessed for late reports. Annual reports are due on or before the 15th day of the 5th month following the organization's year-end. A penalty of $10 will be assessed for late filings.

Taxes:

Taxation and Revenue Department
Post Office Box 25127
Santa Fe, NM 87504-5128
Telephone: 505-827-0700
Web: www.tax.newmexico.gov

The state of New Mexico does provide for an automatic exemption of charitable organizations.

Charitable Solicitation registration:

>Office of the Attorney General
>Charitable Organization Registry
>408 Galisteo Street
>Villagra Building
>Santa Fe, NM 87501

>Or

>Post Office Drawer 1508
>Santa Fe, NM 87504-1508
>Telephone: 505-827-6000
>Web: www.nmag.gov

The state of New Mexico requires that organizations that will be seeking charitable donations register with the Attorney General. Annual renewals are due within six months following the organization's year-end.

NEW YORK

To apply for incorporation:

Department of State
Division of Corporations, State Records, and UCC
One Commerce Plaza
99 Washington Avenue, 6th Floor
Albany, NY 12231
Telephone: 518-473-2492
Telephone: 518-473-1654
FAX: 518-473-1418
Email: corporations@dos.state.ny.us
Web: www.dos.state.ny.us/corps

The state of New York provides fillable forms which can be found at the following link: http://www.dos.ny.gov/forms/corporations/1511-f-l.pdf. The filing fee is $75, payable to the Department of State. Expedited service is available, with fees ranging from an additional $25 to $150 for processing within two hours.

Name reservations can be made for 60 days by submitting a form and paying the fee of $10. The reservation can be extended twice, for a total of 180 days.

Taxes:

New York State Tax Department
Corporate Tax
W A Harriman Campus
Albany, NY 12227
Telephone: 518-485-6027
Web: www.tax.ny.gov

The state of New York does not provide for automatic exemptions for nonprofit organizations. There are several forms to complete for exemption from typical corporate taxes. Start with Form CT-247, which is available on the website.

Charitable Solicitation registration:

New York State Department of Law
Office of the Attorney General
Charities Bureau — Registration Section
120 Broadway
New York, NY 10271
Telephone: 212-416-8401
Web: www.charitiesnys.com/

Nonprofit organizations that will be soliciting donations in the state of New York are required to register with the Attorney General. The initial filing is completed with Form CHAR-410. The filing fee is $25, payable to the New York State Department of Law. Annual renewals are mandated using Form CHAR-500. The filing fees vary based on annual revenue and the organization's net worth. Both forms are available on the website listed above.

NORTH CAROLINA

To apply for incorporation:

> Department of the Secretary of State
> Corporations Division
> 2 South Salisbury Street
> Raleigh, NC 27601

> Or

> Post Office Box 29622
> Raleigh, NC 27226-0622
> Telephone: 919-807-2000
> FAX: 919-807-2039
> Web: www.secretary.state.nc.us/corporations

The state of North Carolina provides forms in PDF, as well as Word format that can be used to fill in your organization's information to be printed and mailed. The filing fee is $60, payable to the Secretary of State.

North Carolina does require corporations to file annual reports and provides pre-printed forms online. Prior to the due date, the organization will receive Form CD-345 by mail. Annual reports should be mailed to:

> Annual Report
> Post Office Box 29525
> Raleigh, NC 29626-0525

Taxes:

> Department of Revenue
> Post Office Box 25000
> Raleigh, NC 27640-0640
> Web: http://www.dornc.com/

North Carolina does not provide an automatic exemption for nonprofit organizations.

Charitable Solicitation registration:

North Carolina Department of the Secretary of State
Solicitation Licensing Section
2 South Salisbury Street
Post Office Box 29622
Raleigh, NC 27626-0622
Telephone: 919-807-2214
Email: csl@sosnc.com

The state of North Carolina requires registration of organizations that will be soliciting donations. The application is available online, as well as the annual report form. The filing fees vary, depending on the amount of contributions. The range of fees is $0 to $200, payable to the North Carolina Department of the Secretary of State.

NORTH DAKOTA

To apply for incorporation:

> Secretary of State
> State of North Dakota
> 600 East Boulevard Avenue, Dept 108, 1st Floor
> Bismarck, ND 58505-0500
> Telephone: 701-328-2900
> FAX: 701-328-2992
> Email: sos@nd.gov
> Web: www.nd.gov/sos/nonprofit/

The state of North Dakota provides all of the required forms on their easy-to-use website. Articles of Incorporation are available at the following link: http://www.nd.gov/eforms/Doc/sfn13003.pdf. The filing fee is $40. Organizational names can be reserved by $10 for a period of 12 months. You will need to complete Form SFN-13015, which is available on their website.

North Dakota requires filing annual reports, which are due by February 1 each year. The initial report is due the year following your organization's date of incorporation. The filing fee is $10 if filed by the due date; late reports require a payment of $15. Checks should be made payable to the Secretary of State. Reports can be faxed with credit card information to (701) 328-2992 or mailed to:

> Annual Report Processing Center
> Secretary of State
> State of North Dakota
> Post Office Box 5513
> Bismarck, ND 58506-5513

Taxes:

> Office of the State Tax Commissioner
> State Tax Department
> 600 East Boulevard Avenue, Dept 127
> Bismarck, ND 58505-0599
> Telephone: 701-328-7088
> FAX: 701-328-3700
> Email: salestax@nd.gov
> Web: www.nd.gov/tax

You will need to apply for sales and use tax exemptions for your organization.

Charitable Solicitation registration:

> Secretary of State
> 600 East Boulevard Avenue
> Bismarck, ND 58505
> Telephone: 701-328-3665
> FAX: 701-328-1690

The state requires charitable organizations to register and file annual reports. The initial registration statement (SFN-11300) has a filing fee of $25. The annual reports (SFN-11302) require a filing fee of $10.

OHIO

To apply for incorporation:

> Secretary of State
> Corporations Division
> 180 East Broad Street, 16th Floor
> Columbus, OH 43215
>
> Or
>
> Client Service Center Counter
> 180 East Broad Street, Suite 103 (Ground Floor)
> Columbus, OH 43215
> Telephone: 877-767-3453
> Email: busserv@ohiosecretaryofstate.gov
> Web: www.ohiosecretaryofstate.gov

The state of Ohio provides sample Articles of Incorporation and Original Appointment of Statutory Agent forms on their website. The filing fee is $125, payable to the Ohio Secretary of State. Expedited services are available as follows: for an additional $100, you will receive processing within two days; for an additional $200, you will receive one business day service; and for an additional $300, you can expect four-hour processing.

Organizational name reservation forms are also available. To reserve your chosen name, complete the online form and submit the filing fee of $50, payable to the Ohio Secretary of State. The reservation is valid for six months.

Ohio requires a statement of continued existence be filed every five years. You will receive written notice from the Ohio Secretary of State. The filing fee is $25. It is also mandated that the statutory agent filing be accurate. If you need to update (change) your organization's statutory agent, the filing fee is $25.

Taxes:

> Ohio Department of Taxation
> Post Office Box 530
> Columbus, OH 43216-0530
> Telephone: 888-405-4039
> Web: www.tax.ohio.gov

The state does provide an automatic exemption.

Charitable Solicitation registration:

> Attorney General
> Charitable Law Section
> 150 East Gay Street, 23rd Floor
> Columbus, OH 43215
> Telephone: 800-282-0515
> FAX: 614-466-9788
> Email: charitablelaw@ohioattorneygeneral.gov
> Web: www.ohioattorneygeneral.gov/about/sections/charitable-law

Registration and annual reports are required by the state of Ohio.

OKLAHOMA

To apply for incorporation:

Secretary of State
Corporation Division
2300 North Lincoln Boulevard, Room 101
State Capitol Building
Oklahoma City, OK 73105-4897
Telephone: 405-521-3912
Web: www.sos.ok.gov

The state of Oklahoma's Secretary of State requires the filing of Articles of Incorporation; a fill-in form is provided at: https://www.sos.ok.gov/forms/FM0008.PDF. The filing fee is $25, payable to the Oklahoma Secretary of State. Same-day service is available for an additional $25. Organizations are also required to file a Designation of Registered Agent form. The filing fee is also $25.

You may call the Business Filing Division at (405) 521-3912 to verify the availability of the chosen name for your organization. You may reserve the name for 60 days for a fee of $10.

Taxes:

Oklahoma Tax Commission
2501 Lincoln Boulevard
Oklahoma City, OK 73194-0009
Telephone: 405-521-3160
Web: www.tax.ok.gov

The state provides for an automatic exemption for charitable organizations.

Charitable Solicitation registration:

Oklahoma Secretary of State
2300 North Lincoln Boulevard
State Capitol Building
Oklahoma City, OK 73105

Your organization will need to complete the following form to register: https://www.sos.ok.gov/forms/FM0104.PDF. The filing fee is $65, payable to the Oklahoma Secretary of State. If the anticipated contributions are less than $10,000, the filing fee is reduced to $15. The state requires an annual report to be submitted on or before the anniversary date of the initial registration.

OREGON

To apply for incorporation:

> Corporation Division
> State of Oregon
> 255 Capitol Street NE, Suite 151
> Salem, OR 97310-1327
> Telephone: 503-986-2200
> FAX: 503-378-4381
> Web: www.filinginoregon.com

The state of Oregon allows new nonprofit organizations to register online or to complete and mail the form found at this link: http://www.filinginoregon.com/pages/forms/business/np_articles.pdf. The filing fee is $50, payable to the Secretary of State. The registration must be renewed annually and the filing fee is $50 each year.

You may reserve the chosen name for your organization by completing the required form and paying a fee of $50.

Taxes:

> Department of Revenue
> 955 Center Street, NE
> Salem, OR 97301-2555
> Telephone: 503-378-4988
> Web: www.oregon.gov/DOR

The state provides automatic exemption for designated charitable organizations.

Charitable Solicitation registration:

> Oregon Department of Justice
> Charitable Activities Section
> 1515 SW 5th Avenue, Suite 410
> Portland, OR 97201-5451
> Telephone: 971-673-1880
> Web: www.doj.state.or.us

Organizations are required to register with the state using Form RF-C. There is no associated registration fee for the initial filing. Annual reports are required and are due 4 ½ months following the organization's year-end. The filing fee varies based on the organization's revenues, ranging from a minimum of $10 up to $200. If the report is filed late, additional penalties will be assessed.

PENNSYLVANIA

To apply for incorporation:

> Pennsylvania Department of State
> Corporation Bureau
> 401 North Street, Room 206
> Harrisburg, PA 17120
>
> Or
>
> Post Office Box 8722
> Harrisburg, PA 17105-8722
> Telephone: 717-787-1057
> Web: www.dos.state.pa.us/corps

Your organization will be required to file Articles of Incorporation and a Docketing Statement. Both forms are available on the Department of State's website. The filing fee is $125, payable to the Department of State.

An annual report is required when there is a change in the corporation's officers. The due date is April 30.

An organization's chosen name can be reserved by submitting the completed form, along with a $70 filing fee. The reservation is valid for 120 days.

Taxes:

> Department of Revenue
> Bureau of Corporation Taxes
> Post Office Box 280427
> Harrisburg, PA 17128-0427
> Telephone: 717-787-1064
> Web: www.revenue.state.pa.us/

The state does not provide an automatic exemption for designated charitable organizations.

Charitable Solicitation registration:

Department of State
Bureau of Charitable Organizations
207 North Office Building
Harrisburg, PA 17120
Telephone: 717-783-1720
FAX: 717-783-6014
Web: http://www.dos.state.pa.us/portal/server.pt/community/bureau_
of_charitable_organizations/12444

Most charitable organizations are required to file Form BCO-10. This form is used for the initial filing, as well as the annual renewals. The filing fee varies based on the organization's gross contributions, ranging from $15 to $250. The fee schedule and exemption listings are included in the instructions for completing the form.

RHODE ISLAND

To apply for incorporation:

> Secretary of State
> 148 West River Street
> Providence, RI 02904-2615
> Telephone: 401-222-2185
> FAX: 401-227-1309
> Email: businessinfo@sos.ri.gov
> Web: www.ri.gov/sos/quickstart/help

The state of Rhode Island has an excellent, easy-to-follow website. The state provides fill-in-the-blank forms for nonprofit Articles of Incorporation. The filing fee is $35, payable to the Rhode Island Secretary of State.

Name requirements are standard—the chosen name of your organization cannot be the same or deceptively similar to any other corporation. You may search for availability by using the state's search tool at: http://ucc.state.ri.us/corpsearch/corpsearchinput.asp. You may also call 401-222-3040 to inquire about availability.

Rhode Island does require the filing of an annual report.

Taxes:

> State of Rhode Island and Providence Plantations
> Department of Revenue
> Field Audit Section
> One Capitol Hill
> Providence, RI 02908
> Telephone: 401-277-2905
> FAX: 401-277-6006

Charitable Solicitation registration:

> Department of Business Regulations
> Securities Division
> Charitable Organization Section
> 1511 Pontiac Avenue
> John O. Pastore Complex Building, 69-1
> Cranston, RI 02920
> Telephone: 401-462-9583

The state requires the registration submission to be on a CD-ROM. The filing fee is $90, payable to the General Treasurer, State of Rhode Island. You will be required to file an annual report in Rhode Island.

SOUTH CAROLINA

To apply for incorporation:

> State of South Carolina
> Secretary of State
> Public Charities Division
> 1205 Pendleton Street, Suite 525
> Columbia, SC 29201
> Telephone: 803-734-1790
> FAX: 803-734-1604
> Email: charities@sos.sc.gov
> Web: www.scbos.sc.gov/scboslibrary/business_resources.aspx

South Carolina's Secretary of State's website is extremely user-friendly. The state provides fill-in-the-blank Articles of Incorporation for your convenience. The filing fee is $50, payable to the Secretary of State.

Annual reports are required by the Secretary of State. There is not an associated filing fee. The report is due by the 15th day of the 5th month after the end of the corporation's fiscal year.

Taxes:

> South Carolina Department of Revenue
> 301 Gervais Street
> Post Office Box 125
> Columbia, SC 29214
> Telephone: 803-898-5445
> FAX: 803-898-5020
> Web: www.sctax.org/default.htm

Charitable Solicitation registration:

> State of South Carolina
> Secretary of State
> Public Charities Division
> 1205 Pendleton Street, Suite 525
> Columbia, SC 29201
> Telephone: 803-734-1790
> FAX: 803-734-1604
> Email: charities@sos.sc.gov
> Web: www.scbos.sc.gov/scboslibrary/business_resources.aspx

Organizations with gross revenues of less than $5,000 are exempt from registering. All required organizations must register annually.

SOUTH DAKOTA

To apply for incorporation:

> Office of the Secretary of State
> State Capitol
> 500 East Capitol Street
> Pierre, SD 57501
> Telephone: 605-773-4845
> FAX: 605-773-4550
> Web: http://sos.sd.gov

Like most other states, South Dakota provides online fill-in-the-blank Articles of Incorporation. The filing fee for nonprofit corporations is $30, payable to the Secretary of State. For an additional fee of $50, the state provides expedited service.

To reserve your chosen name, the state requires a reservation fee of $25.

South Dakota does require corporations, including nonprofit, to file an annual report. The filing fee is $10 annually.

Taxes:

> Department of Revenue
> 445 East Capitol Avenue
> Pierre, SD 57501
> Telephone: 605-773-3311
> FAX: 605-773-6729
> Web: www.state.sd.us

Charitable organizations receive an automatic exemption.

Charitable Solicitation registration:

> South Dakota Attorney General
> 1302 East Highway 14, Suite 1
> Pierre, SD 57501-8501
> Telephone: 605-773-3215
> Email: atghelp@state.sd.us
> Web: http://atg.sd.gov/

The state does not provide an exemption for nonprofit organizations with gross revenues under $5,000.

TENNESSEE

To apply for incorporation:

> State of Tennessee
> Department of State
> Corporate Filings
> 312 Rosa L. Parks Avenue
> William R. Snodgrass Tower, 6th Floor
> Nashville, TN 37243
> Telephone: 615-741-2286
> Web: http://www.tn.gov/sos/bus_svc/

The state provides fill-in-the-blank Articles of Incorporation. The filing fee is $100, payable to the Division of Business Services. Annual reports are required by the state of Tennessee.

You may reserve the name you've chosen for your organization for a fee of $20.

Taxes:

> Tennessee Department of Revenue
> Andrew Jackson Office Building
> 500 Deaderick Street
> Nashville, TN 37242
> Telephone: 615-253-0600
> Web: www.tennesseeanytime.org/bizreg

Charitable Solicitation registration:

> State of Tennessee
> Department of State
> Division of Charitable Solicitation and Gaming
> 312 Rosa L. Parks Avenue
> William R. Snodgrass Tower, 8th Floor
> Nashville, TN 37243
> Telephone: 615-741-2286
> FAX: 615-253-5173
> Web: http://www.tn.gov/sos/charity/

Organizations with annual gross revenue in excess of $30,000 are required to file an annual report. The filing fee is $50.

TEXAS

To apply for incorporation:

> Secretary of State
> Corporation Division
> Post Office Box 13697
> Austin, TX 78711-3697
> Telephone: 512-463-5555
> FAX: 512-463-5709
> Web: www.sos.state.tx.us/corp/nonprofitorg.shtml

The state of Texas provides Form 202, Nonprofit Corporation Summary, to help you draft your own Articles of Incorporation. The filing fee of $25 should be made payable to the Secretary of State.

Organizations are required to file a report once every four years. The SOS will notify organizations before the due date.

To verify name availability, you may call 512-463-5555. Reservation of your organization's chosen name will cost you $40, for a period of 120 days.

Taxes:

> Office of the Comptroller
> Exempt Organizations Section
> Post Office Box 13528
> Austin, TX 78711-3528
> Telephone: 800-252-5555 or
> Telephone: 512-463-4600

Charitable Solicitation registration:

> Attorney General
> Charitable Trusts Section
> Consumer Protection Division
> Post Office Box 12548
> Austin, TX 78711-2548
> Telephone: 512-463-2100
> FAX: 512-475-2994
> Web: www.oag.state.tx.us/consumer/nonprofits.shtml

At this time, the state of Texas does not require charitable organizations or professional fundraisers to register with the state.

UTAH

To apply for incorporation:

> Department of Commerce
> Division of Corporations
> Post Office Box 45801
> Salt Lake City, UT 84111
> Telephone: 801-530-4849 or
> Telephone: 877-526-3994
> FAX: 801-530-6438
> Email: corpucc@utah.gov
> Web: http://corporations.utah.gov

Guidelines are provided by the state to help you draft your Articles of Incorporation. The filing fee is $30, payable to the State of Utah. For expedited service, you will pay an additional $75.

Name reservation and registration are both $22.

The state requires charitable organizations to file annual reports. The filing fee is $10, if filed on time. Late reports have a $20 filing fee.

Taxes:

> Utah State Tax Commission
> 210 N. 1950 West
> Salt Lake City, UT 84134
> Telephone: 801-297-2200
> FAX: 801-297-7699
> Web: http://tax.utah.gov/

Charitable Solicitation registration:

> Department of Commerce
> Division of Consumer Protection
> 160 East 300 South
> Salt Lake City, UT 84111
> Telephone: 801-530-6601
> FAX: 801-530-6001
> Email: consumerprotection@utah.gov
> Web: www.consumerprotection.utah.gov/

The state of Utah requires registration and annual filings from charitable organizations and professional fundraisers. The fee is $100.

VERMONT

To apply for incorporation:

> Secretary of State
> 128 State Street
> Montpelier, VT 05633-1104
> Telephone: 802-828-2386
> FAX: 802-828-2853
> Web: www.sec.state.vt.us

Vermont provides user-friendly fill-in-the-blank Articles of Incorporation forms for your use. The filing fee is $75, payable to the Vermont Secretary of State.

Name reservations can be made for a fee of $20. The reservation will be valid for 120 days.

Nonprofit corporations must file biennial reports and pay a filing fee of $15.

Taxes:

> Department of Taxes
> Agency of Administration
> 133 State Street
> Montpelier, VT 05633-1401
> Telephone: 802-828-2551
> FAX: 802-828-5787

The state doesn't provide an automatic exemption for nonprofit organizations.

Charitable Solicitation registration:

> Office of the Attorney General
> 109 State Street
> Montpelier, VT 05609-1001
> Telephone: 802-828-3171
> Web: www.atg.state.vt.us

VIRGINIA

To apply for incorporation:

> State Corporation Commission
> Tyler Building, 1st Floor
> 1300 E. Main Street
> Richmond, VA 23219 or
> Post Office Box 1197
> Richmond, VA 23218
> Telephone: 804-371-9733
> Web: www.scc.virginia.gov

The state provides required forms on their website. Nonprofit organizations (non-stock corporation) will file for SCC819. The filing fee is $75, payable to the State Corporation Commission.

Annual reports are required by the state. You will receive notification via postal mail.

Taxes:

> Department of Taxation
> Post Office Box 1115
> Richmond, VA 23218 or
> 1957 Westmoreland Street
> Richmond, VA 23230
> FAX: 804-254-6113
> Web: www.tax.virginia.gov

Charitable Solicitation registration:

> Office of the Virginia Department of Agriculture and Consumer Services
> Post Office Box 526
> Richmond, VA 23218-0526
> Telephone: 804-786-1343
> FAX: 804-225-2666
> Web: www.vdacs.virginia.gov

The registration fee for a new organization with no prior financial history is $100. The fee is payable to the Treasurer of Virginia. The subsequent registration statements have a filing fee between $30 and $325, depending on the gross revenues. Please see the website for a listing of exemptions.

WASHINGTON

To apply for incorporation:

> Washington Secretary of State
> Charities Program
> 801 Capitol Way South
> Post Office Box 40234
> Olympia, WA 98504-0234
> Telephone: 360-725-0378
> Web: www.sos.wa.gov/charities

The state provides fill-in-the-blank Articles of Incorporation on their website. The filing fee is $30, payable to the Secretary of State.

Annual reports are required to be submitted prior to the 15th of the 5th month after the organization's year-end. The original filing fee is $60 and all subsequent renewal reports will require a fee of $40.

Taxes:

> Washington State Department of Revenue
> Post Office Box 47476
> Olympia, WA 98504-7476
> Telephone: 800-647-7706
> Web: http://dor.wa.gov/

Nonprofit organizations receive an automatic exemption.

Charitable Solicitation registration:

> Washington Secretary of State
> Charities Program
> 801 Capitol Way South
> Post Office Box 40234
> Olympia, WA 98504-0234
> Telephone: 360-725-0378
> Email: charities@sos.wa.gov
> Web: www.sos.wa.gov/charities

The initial registration fee is $300 and annual renewals will be $225.

WEST VIRGINIA

To apply for incorporation:

> Secretary of State
> 1900 Kanawha Boulevard East
> Building1, Suite 157-K
> Charleston, WV 25305
> Telephone: 304-558-8000
> FAX: 304-558-5758
> Email: business@wvsos.com
> Web: www.sos.wv.gov

In order to file the fill-in-the-blank Articles of Incorporation, you will need to pay a registration fee of $25. Your check should be payable to the West Virginia Secretary of State.

A name reservation can be obtained by filing the application and paying a fee of $15. The reservation is valid for 120 days. You may fax your application (available online) to 304-558-8381.

West Virginia requires charitable organizations to file annual reports.

Taxes:

> West Virginia State Tax Department
> Taxpayer Service Division
> Post Office Box 3784
> Charleston, WV 25337-3784
> Telephone: 304-558-3333
> Web: http://www.wva.state.wv.us

Charitable Solicitation registration:

> Secretary of State
> 1900 Kanawha Boulevard East
> Building 1, Suite 157-K
> Charleston, WV 25305
> Telephone: 304-558-8000
> FAX: 304-558-5758
> Email: business@wvsos.com
> Web: www.sos.wv.gov

Charitable organizations that will be soliciting donations in West Virginia are required to register. The filing fee is $15 for organizations with gross revenues under $1 million and $50 for those with revenues over $1 million.

WISCONSIN

To apply for incorporation:

> Department of Financial Institutions
> Division of Corporate and Consumer Services
> 345 West Washington Avenue
> Madison, WI 53703
> Telephone: 608-261-7577
> FAX: 608-267-6813
> Web: www.wdfi.org/corporations/

The state of Wisconsin provides fill-in-the-blank Articles of Incorporation. Submit completed forms with a fee of $35, payable to the Department of Financial Institutions. You may add an additional $25 for expedited service.

You may reserve the name you have chosen for your organization by calling 608-261-7577. The reservation fee is $10 and the fee for registration of your organization's name is $25.

In addition, the state of Wisconsin requires organizations to file annual reports. The filing fee is $10.

Taxes:

> Department of Revenue
> 2135 Rimrock Road
> Madison, WI 53713
> Telephone: 608-266-2772
> FAX: 608-267-0834
> Web: www.revenue.wi.gov

Charitable organizations are granted an automatic exemption.

Charitable Solicitation registration:

> State of Wisconsin
> Department of Safety and Professional Services
> Post Office Box 8935
> Madison, WI 53708-8935
> Telephone: 608-266-2112 or
> Telephone: 877-617-1565
> FAX: 608-261-7083
> Web: http://drl.wi.gov

The fee to file the initial credential application is $15, payable to the Department of Safety and Professional Services.

WYOMING

To apply for incorporation:

> Secretary of State
> Business Division
> State Capitol Building, Room 106
> 200 West 24th Street
> Cheyenne, WY 82002-0020
> Telephone: 307-777-7311
> FAX: 307-777-5339
> Email: business@wyo.gov
> Web: http://soswy.state.wy.us/

The state of Wyoming provides fill-in-the-blank Articles of Incorporation, along with instructions. The filing fee is $25, payable to the Wyoming Secretary of State.

Your chosen name can be reserved for 120 days for a fee of $10.

Annual reports are required by Wyoming's Secretary of State. The initial filing and subsequent reports require a fee of $25.

Taxes:

> Department of Revenue
> Herschler Building, 2nd Floor West
> Cheyenne, WY 82002-0110
> Telephone: 307-777-7961
> Email: directorofrevenue@wyo.gov
> Web: http://revenue.state.wy.us/

Charitable Solicitation registration:

> Office of the Attorney General
> Consumer Protection Division
> State Capitol Building
> 1515 North Flagler Drive, Suite 900
> Cheyenne, WY 82002
> Telephone: 307-777-7378

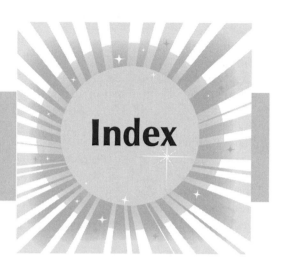

Index

101 SERIES

Create the perfect résumé. Ace the interview. Hone your skills. Books in the *101* series provide complete "get the job" advice from career experts for anyone seeking new employment. Tips are presented in an easy-to-read, pithy format, and each book is only $12.99 so getting the new job doesn't have to break the bank!

101 GREAT RÉSUMÉS
THIRD EDITION
1-59863-855-6 • $12.99 • 216 PGS

101 WAYS TO MAKE YOURSELF INDISPENSABLE AT WORK
1-4354-5432-4 • $12.99 • 208 PGS

101 SMART QUESTIONS TO ASK ON YOUR INTERVIEW
THIRD EDITION
1-59863-854-8 • $12.99 • 168 PGS

101 GREAT ANSWERS TO THE TOUGHEST INTERVIEW QUESTIONS SIXTH EDITION
1-59863-853-X • $12.99 • 200 PGS

90 DAYS TO SUCCESS SERIES

The first three months on the job are the most important! For those who have already landed the job and are eager to hit the ground running from Day 1, we provide the *90 Days to Success* series. These books provide expert advice and action plans for achievement from executives who have been in your shoes before and want to share their considerable experience.

90 DAYS TO SUCCESS AS A MANAGER
1-59863-865-3 • $19.99 • 232 PGS

90 DAYS TO SUCCESS AS A PROJECT MANAGER
1-59863-869-6 • $19.99 • 376 PGS

90 DAYS TO SUCCESS IN FUNDRAISING
1-59863-876-9 • $19.99 • 272 PGS

90 DAYS TO SUCCESS IN CONSULTING
1-4354-5442-1 • $19.99 • 336 PGS

90 DAYS TO SUCCESS IN GRANT WRITING
1-4354-5486-3 • $19.99 • 272 PGS

PERSPECTIVES™ SERIES

Ever wonder what your clients, customers, or employees *really* think of the job you're doing? Find out with the *Perspectives*™ series. In *Perspectives*, two or more successful executives share their opinions, but never collaborate, ensuring unbiased and unfiltered views of business topics such as increasing sales, building brands, marketing tactics, and managing employees. The frank "he said/she said" format of these books provides a unique learning experience as well as an entertaining read!

PERSPECTIVES ON INCREASING SALES
1-59863-874-2 • $29.99 • 311 PGS

PERSPECTIVES ON BRANDING
1-59863-872-6 • $29.99 • 276 PGS

PERSPECTIVES ON MANAGING EMPLOYEES
1-59863-873-4 • $29.99 • 300 PGS

PERSPECTIVES ON MARKETING
1-59863-871-8 • $29.99 • 377 PGS